Best Wishes,

Dan Brannan

Everyday Angels

by Dan Brannan

D1377996

Printed in the United States of America

First Edition – July 1996

ISBN 0-9650228-3-8

Published by Dan Brannan Publications
P.O. Box 1708
Seneca, SC   29679

Printed by Faith Printing
Taylors, SC

Cover design by Bryan Lee and Dana Alder

About The Author

Dan Brannan has been in the field of journalism since 1978, when he enrolled as a journalism and psychology major at Eastern Illinois University. Following his 1982 graduation from EIU, he began his professional career as a sports writer for *The Shelbyville Daily Union* in Shelbyville, Ill., a rural farming community in central Illinois. Three years later, he joined Thomson Newspapers, becoming a sports writer at the *Mt. Vernon Register-News* in Mt. Vernon, Ill., a mid-sized town in southern Illinois, quickly moving up to the sports editor position.

In 1988, at age 27, he was named managing editor of *The Standard•Democrat* in the small southeast Missouri town of Sikeston. During his tenure, the paper's subscription rate rocketed by nearly 20 percent, the top single percentage increase in the nation as ranked by *Delivering the News* magazine in their August 1990 issue.

The Thomson chain promoted him to managing editor of *The Evening Telegram* in Rocky Mount, N.C., in April 1990. Rocky Mount is an industrial and rural town of about 50,000. It lies in eastern North Carolina about an hour east of Raleigh, the state capital.

Brannan guided *The Telegram* to historic circulation highs and gained both national and international prominence for his work. He appeared in stories in *Presstime* magazine in the May 1992 issue and in *The Financial Post* of Toronto that same spring.

His honors at Rocky Mount included a Thomson Newspapers Award of Excellence in 1991; directing a first-place award from the North Carolina Press Association for best investigative reporting; the North Carolina Associated Press' Parker Award for Meritorious Service; and the North Carolina American Lung Association award for meritorious service in 1991-92 and 1992-93. The Southern Newspaper Association honored the paper in 1992 for Brannan's development of a weekly educational section.

Brannan left *The Telegram* in October 1993 to start his own weekly newspaper, *The Bridge.* Brannan sold his interests in the paper in December 1994 and moved to Clemson/Seneca, S.C., where he became editor of the *Journal/Tribune* and *The Messenger.*

The Clemson/Seneca area is mostly rural in nature, with Clemson University providing opportunities in higher education.

Brannan led the *Journal/Tribune* to the South Carolina Press Association General Excellence Award for 1995 in the Two- or Three-Times-Weekly division, signifying the paper as being the best in the state in its division.

Brannan also led the papers to a first-place award in Best Special Section; third in Community Service; and third in Business Reporting with a weekly business column. Brannan was honored in 1995 by the South Carolina Department of Health and Environmental Control with a state-wide award for health promotion.

Recently, Brannan wrote a book chronicling his struggle with diabetes and the stories of others coping with diabetes entitled *Life To The Fullest: Stories Of People Coping With Diabetes.* The book been reviewed and approved by the board of directors of the national American Diabetes Association office in Alexandria, Va. The book is being distributed nationally in bookstores. Brannan has also written a children's book about diabetes, accompanied with a cassette tape, called *Look! Listen! Learn!: Ways For Kids To Cope With Diabetes.*

Brannan was elected president of the American Diabetes Association's Piedmont Region in 1996. In the previous year, he served as advisory board chairman for The Salvation Army in Oconee County. Brannan continually speaks about his experiences with diabetes, adamant about spreading his positive message to both children and adults.

Today, Brannan is 35 and entering his 14th year in professional journalism.

Table of Contents

B. K. Seabolt

Dedication

Shortly after I arrived at the *Journal/Tribune* and *The Messenger* in Clemson/Seneca, S.C., in the fall of 1994, I became intrigued by a young person I knew only as B.K.

B.K. was a friendly, helpful, happy individual. I saw him pass by my desk many times after I arrived, and I wanted to know more about him.

What I soon learned about Brian Keith Seabolt inspired me to assemble this collection of columns and stories I had written during my work in several communities across the United States.

I described B.K. in a column as "an angel in disguise." He had experienced a traumatic childhood, surviving a serious auto accident.

B.K.'s strong spirit helps countless people every day throughout the community, and if it had not been for a place called the Collins Children's Home, B.K.'s story wouldn't have had such a happy ending.

The Collins Home takes in underprivileged children from across the state of South Carolina and gives them a warm, loving, stable environment. Founded in 1980 by Joe and Anne Rackley, the home, located in Seneca, S.C., has been an icon of the community ever since it started.

More than 100 children whose lives seemed hopeless have been helped by Joe and Anne and the Collins Children's Home volunteers over the years.

A portion of the proceeds from this book will help the Collins Children's Home build more cottages to accommodate additional children. It is to these children that this book is dedicated.

Foreword

Inspiration is difficult to absorb in heavy doses. You may find this hard to believe, but my first draft of this manuscript contained 60 inspirational stories.

I tested my creation on a person with a doctorate in education and two top executives in the publishing industry.

One of the publishing experts wrote, "The number of stories is overwhelming. One can only absorb so much inspiration at one sitting. *Everyday Angels* has some great human-interest stories about very special people. Perhaps I would have gotten more out of the stories if I had read each of them a few days apart.

"With apologies to Forrest Gump, it was like eating a whole box of fine chocolates at one sitting - one's taste is numbed after the first several pieces. One or two a day would be more palatable."

At that point, I trimmed the amount of stories in half.

Within each story, you will find a quote for the day. I hope you will think about that quote and the story. Then on day two, move on to the next story, and so on.

You may become so involved in the lives of my "angels" that you read ahead, but I recommend one a day for 30 days. Of course, there may be some stories in this book you will want to read again and again. Just make sure this book is placed where it belongs, in your living room, by the bed or wherever you enjoy reading, not stacked away on a bookshelf collecting dust.

Share the book with your family, friends and neighbors. I think it would make excellent bedtime stories for the kids.

Who knows, the book may just inspire the angel in you.

Happy reading!

Introduction

There has been a lot of discussion about angels in recent years, with several books and songs released on the subject.

I know angels are all around us, and often in places where we don't exactly expect them.

I believe my own life has been saved nearly a half-dozen times by a higher power. I developed pneumonia at a young age and could have died, but survived.

Starting at age 33, I experienced my closest call with death. I developed diabetes in the winter of 1994 and lost about 45 pounds in a three-month span. I was so weak and fatigued I could barely walk up a flight of stairs without having to take a nap. And to think I had run two 26.2-mile marathons not so long before!

I had several other occasions during the last two years where I believe there was special intervention on my behalf.

The first occurred when a physician in Rocky Mount, N.C., persuaded me to overcome my terror of needles and inject insulin into my body each day. After speaking with an aunt and much discussion with a friend who was an insulin-dependent diabetic, I decided to go on insulin. If I had not started taking insulin, I would have died.

My next close call occurred one day when my blood sugar had dropped after exercising at lunchtime. I had swum too far and forgotten my lunch.

I ended up driving in the Oconee County (S.C.) mountain area, with winding roads and several-thousand-foot dropoffs below. A woman saw me, followed me and eventually got me to stop.

After discovering I was a person with diabetes, she quickly got some orange juice for me. Without her help, there is no doubt I would have gone over the cliff or hit another car in the opposite lane.

Another time, my blood sugar dropped while I was running and I collapsed. I was fortunate that someone was with me at the time and tended to me by getting a ride back to the house and some orange juice into my system.

The next close encounter occurred when I took a nap one Sunday afternoon and failed to wake up. My blood sugar had dropped during the day and continued on down. If an alert friend had not stopped by, roused me and fed me some pizza, I could have lapsed into a diabetic coma.

After the last encounter and another emergency room visit, I was eager to seek the advice of a medical specialist. Paul Davidson, a diabetes specialist in Atlanta, has probably added years to my future because of his expertise on treatment methods.

I now test my blood sugar four times a day and take four insulin injections a day. My weight has returned and I am able to function efficiently in my life. Some may wonder how a person can stick eight needles in the fingers and stomach a day and stand it.

I can only say I do it because of the help and grace of God. I feel blessed to open my eyes each day and see another sunrise and another opportunity to enjoy life.

There are many everyday angels, some who simply help people and others who have overcome great odds to inspire.

Inside this book, you'll read the stories of people like:

• **Anne and Joe Rackley**, the founders of a South Carolina children's home which takes in underprivileged, abused, neglected or abandoned children and gives them a loving, stable environment.

• **Tony Sample**, who was my best friend for many years and didn't allow a deformed arm to stop him from becoming a champion athlete, husband and father.

- **Mike Rodgers**, a Salvation Army lieutenant who battled back from a truck accident that came very close to killing him. He has brought vigor to The Salvation Army's mission in Oconee County, S.C.

- **Jake Einhorn,** an executive with New York-based Saks Fifth Avenue who returned the wallet of a South Carolina teen-age girl, which she had lost while on a school trip to The Big Apple.

- **Billy Mills**, the winner of the 10,000-meter gold medal at the 1964 Tokyo Olympics who continues to give back to his people and to communities across the nation.

- **Anna Marie Davidson**, who was born and immediately abandoned in Vietnam, yet has brought an immense amount of sunshine to her adopted South Carolina family.

- **Adam Rumoshosky,** who used his experience in the Keep America Beautiful program to start a similar program in his adopted hometown - a program which has proven to be an unequaled success.

- **Joe Stokley**, who had part of his face blown off by a gunshot, yet learned to talk again and became a successful teacher, husband and father of four.

- **Donna Gustavel**, born with cerebral palsy, who has overcome great odds to help and inspire many other people with her kindheartedness.

- **Norman Lambert,** owner of Lambert's Cafe in Sikeston and Branson, Mo., who has a heart of gold for his employees and customers.

- **Nick and Mayo Boddie,** founders of Boddie-Noell Enterprises, which owns and operates many of the Hardee's Restaurants in the United States. The Boddies have encountered great professional success, but have never forgotten their roots.

- **Evelyn Coggins,** over 80 years old, who followed her lifelong dream to learn how to play the violin despite having heart problems.

- **Warren Detrick**, a businessman who created the white marking board that is now standard equipment in most offices, schools and homes.

Warren also has a special love for children.

You will find many additional stories which will inspire you, make you think and realize that angels are all around us; all you have to do is look for them.

These everyday angels were selected from people I have encountered in Illinois, Missouri, North Carolina and South Carolina in nearly a decade and a half of working in the newspaper business.

All of them have meant something to me, to their communities and to their families over the years. Their stories have inspired me and helped me to realize that things do happen for a reason.

I hope they will inspire you, as well.

Dan Brannan
Seneca, SC
June 1996

"You probably did die, but I think you went to heaven and God brought you back to be an angel on earth."

- Warren Detrick on B.K. Seabolt

DAY 1
An Angel in Disguise

Brian Keith Seabolt first laid eyes on Anne Rackley, the co-founder and executive director of the Collins Children's Home in Seneca, S.C., back in 1981.

He promptly asked Anne if he could call her "mother" during their first week together.

"She said yes," he said, "and has been the best mother I've ever had since."

Seabolt, known today as B.K., went through a lot in his early life, but the home, well-known in the Upstate of South Carolina as a place where deserving youngsters can find a warm, loving place, gave him a new lease on life. The Rackleys, Anne and Joe, provided B.K. with a home, education and a purpose.

In fact, B.K. believes that, without the efforts of the Rackleys, his life would more than likely be in ruins.

At age 11, B.K. was involved in a horrifying auto accident that killed his grandfather and nearly left him dead. B.K. was pronounced dead on arrival at the hospital, but somehow revived.

It was touch-and-go for several weeks following the crash; he suffered brain damage and paralysis to one side of his body. He eventually recovered enough to be released from the hospital and was taken in by his natural father.

But for B.K., the nightmare was just beginning. The abuse and emotional neglect he suffered afterward was equally as traumatic as the tragic auto accident, according to this brave young man.

Needless to say, B.K. arrived at the Collins Children's Home confused, his life in tatters, his spirit broken and his heart shattered.

How could you blame him? He'd already been badly injured in a car crash, then went through the experience of not belonging anywhere.

How could a child *not* be affected by what happened?

B.K. had to learn to use his body and mind all over again. Without the devoted efforts of the Rackleys and the home, it is very doubtful he ever would have made it all the way back.

Seneca's Warren Detrick, one of the most ardent supporters of the home, says he has always admired B.K.

"I'm so appreciative of B.K.," he told me. "His enthusiasm, smile and ability to listen are wonderful. He is a goodwill ambassador for the home."

Meeting B.K. is a guarantee to brighten anyone's day, Detrick believes. "He never asks for anything back."

B.K. has worked hard to help build up the home's newspaper recycling program. (The *Journal/Tribune* of Seneca, S.C., is one of many newspapers that recycles its used newsprint each year; much of its waste newsprint to be recycled goes to the Collins Home.)

In fact, thanks in large part to his efforts, newspaper recycling is one of the home's leading fund-raisers, something very important to the facility, which exists solely on the contributions of individuals, churches, clubs and businesses in the area.

B.K.'s smile is infectious. When a person sees a big grin on B.K.'s face and hears a kind comment, it can't help but brighten the day. B.K. is always in good spirits and always has a kind word to say, regardless of the circumstances.

Anne beams with pride and joy when she talks about B.K. She recalled he lacked motivation when he first arrived, walked with an exaggerated limp and could not use his right hand. Thanks to proper supervision and a nurturing home, B.K. no longer has the limp and has regained use of his hand.

"I'm glad he calls me mother; he's the only one at the home who does," Anne said. "That is very special to him."

To the other children of the Collins Home, Anne is known as "mom" or "Mama Anne."

"B.K. is really outgoing and likes being a helper," Anne told me.

I first noticed B.K. at the newspaper office when he came to pick up waste paper, but I only recently learned about his story.

One day, I found my hands completely full when I was in a hurry to make a speech before a local civic club. I looked for some help, and there was B.K., who extended his hands to me and helped me carry things to my car.

"I'm always willing to give someone a helping hand," said B.K. as he walked away from me.

Detrick believes B.K. may well be an angel in disguise.

"I told him once, 'B.K., you probably did die, but I think you went to heaven and God brought you back to be an angel on earth,'" he said.

"Sometimes, it's emotionally draining. I pour out and I pour out; at times, I'm very tired... Then a child comes up and gives me a genuine hug and tells me he or she loves me. It's like magic."
- **Anne Rackley, one of the founders of the Collins Children's Home**

DAY 2
The Story of The Collins Kids

On Valentine's Day 1996, Anne Rackley received 14 yellow roses, one from each of her 14 children.

Anne and her husband, Joe, haven't conceived 14 kids by themselves - Kimberly, age 26, is their only natural daughter - but these 14 kids are more than willing to consider Anne and Joe like their mother and father.

You see, the Rackleys are the founders and directors of the Roxie Anna Collins Children's Home Ministry, Inc., of Seneca, S.C., a place where abused, neglected and abandoned children can find a warm, caring, loving home. It is a place where families are healed in their hearts.

"I especially love yellow roses," Anne told me during my visit to the home that day. Nineteen-year-old Patricia, beaming with pride, handed Anne the flowers.

Patricia is typical of what has transpired at the home since it opened in 1980. She currently attends college, but more than likely would not have had much of a chance if Mama Anne and Daddy Joe had not brought her into their home when she was just 5. "Patricia's mother couldn't take care of her at the time," Anne said. "She was a very scared and quiet little girl when she came into the home, but now, she bubbles with enthusiasm about life."

Many people are supposedly given divine visions of what they should do with their lives. The Rackleys say it was through divine intervention that they came up with the idea to start the home.

Joe was an engineer and Anne was working in administration in the golf business in Pinehurst, N.C., when the calling for the home came. "Even though we made enough money to live very comfortably," Anne told me, "we decided that wasn't all we wanted for the rest of our lives. Everything we have, God gave us. After eight months of serious praying, Joe came to me and said, 'I know what the Lord wants us to do.'

"He told me he had known it for a couple of weeks, but he thought I would think he was crazy when he told me the idea."

Joe then unveiled his vision to Anne of what would become the Collins Children's Home. Originally, the couple had envisioned five cottages, an administration building and a dining hall for the home, which was the "traditional" children's home.

But that just didn't jive with their hope that it would be family-oriented, a place where children could receive as much individual attention as possible. The Rackleys then decided to construct a seven-bedroom home near the Bounty Land community in Seneca and opened their doors to children.

"We knew we had to do it," Anne said. "The community may not have understood the need and that this (project) could be done entirely by the community. All of our funding is private; we had to first prove ourselves by using our personal home and our personal resources. It has always been an act of faith.

"The first few years were tight. I worked at Clemson University for income while Joe was clearing the land and constructing the house. Our daughter, Kimberly, was 10 when we started the home. She just loves her brothers and sisters."

As Anne took me through their home, I was amazed at the neatness of each room. Everything was in place. We spent a lot of time in the study hall room, which used to be the Rackley's garage. It was converted so there would be more room, with many study aids available for the children.

Renae was the first resident of the home in December 1980 at age 8. Three months later, after the home was completed, the home was full of children and has remained that way ever since.

The children are educated in both the Oconee County (S.C.) public schools and at Oconee Christian Academy in Seneca. Anne says that both the public and private school systems have been very good to the children.

The Rackleys chose the name Roxie Anna Collins Children's Home in memory of Joe's grandmother, who lived to the age of 93. "She lived her whole life near Westminster (S.C.)," Anne said. "She had the greatest influence on her family through her generous love and values and trans-ferred those qualities to Joe.

"We wanted to teach our children the same things she taught her children and grandchildren."

Anne looked up to the heavens and said, "I believe Granny Collins knows what we're doing; she knows."

"Collins Kids," as they are sometimes called, come to the home by way of referrals from the South Carolina Department of Social Services, mental health agencies, school systems and private referrals from families. Because the home is so well-thought of, there is always a waiting list for children to get inside. Not all the children there have been abused; some just need a home or help with emotional or behavioral problems.

One of the key things Joe and Anne attempt to do at the home is to look for positive aspects of the children's family situations, even if the parents can't visit the child. Anne recognizes that there is a natural bond between children and their natural parents. "One of the first things chil-dren do after being denied visitation of a family member for years is to find them," Anne said. "Why should we destroy an attempt to build a positive relationship?

"We have many cases where the parents of the children have made progress enough to continue their relationship with their children, with our help. All that some of the fathers and mothers need is confidence in themselves and parental training. They need a friend who believes they can become successful parents."

Anne and Joe are devoted to leading Christian lives and setting good examples for the kids. "We are very serious about our responsibility to live a Christian life," Anne said. "We all go to church together. We have family devotions every morning at 6:30 a.m.; we've found that's the best time to have devotionals. Otherwise, we get so busy, we might not get it done. Our more active children are usually calmer early in the morning, too.

"All the children help to cook and clean in the home and share responsibilities. We post a schedule of who assists with the cooking and cleaning each day."

The home also employs a card system for the children to help them learn self-control. The system starts at green; if a child progresses to yellow, it is time to slow down. Pink means he or she needs to be careful. Orange means to use caution, while blue means a child will lose privileges. The children start each day with the cards on green and all mistakes forgiven.

Anne says it's not always easy being the mother of so many children. "Sometimes, it's emotionally draining," she said. "I pour out and pour out; at times, I'm very tired. I take on all the children's problems, plus get calls all the time from other parents with problems. I understand their needs and want to be helpful.

"Then a child comes up and gives me a genuine hug and tells me he or she loves me. It's like therapy."

Anne's own mother told her she was destined to be a mother. Anne had to help take care of her sisters from the time she was 6 years old, changing diapers and getting their bottles. By 12, Anne was doing all the meal planning and preparation, grocery shopping and house cleaning while her mother worked to support four daughters.

Anne's only break was Sunday lunch, when her mother prepared the meal. That has led to a tradition of having a big Sunday lunch following church services. Sunday lunch is just one of the many family traditions Joe and Anne have passed on to their children.

Joe, like Anne, sometimes has as much stress as he can take. "I remember one little girl who came to the home when she was 8 years old. She had one of the most profane mouths I've ever heard in my life," Joe recalled. "We talked to her hours and hours about it, and she still called us every name in the book.

"Finally, one time, she looked up at me, and gruffly asked, 'What do you want me to call you?'

"I asked, 'What do you want to call me?' She cautiously said, 'Daddy.'"

Joe said "All right, if that's what you want to call me," and she put her arms around his neck and held him for a long time. Then she said, "I've been needing a good daddy for a long time!"

One of the brightest moments at the home was reuniting young Shannon with her brother, Justin, after a six-year separation. Anne had been looking for Justin by contacting Social Services in Kansas all over the area in which Shannon previously lived and stumbled upon a lady who had been Justin's caseworker for the previous three years. The children were reunited at the home for a special week-long visit.

This past year, Joe and Anne were recognized with the South Carolina Order of the Palmetto award, the state's highest honor awarded to a private citizen, by then-Gov. Carroll Campbell. They have also received several Service to Mankind Awards from area Sertoma Clubs.

Not only have the Rackleys cared for more than 50 children in residence at the home, they have helped the community in an outreach program, working with more than another 50 children and their families. The couple has saved many lives from poverty, abuse and neglect.

The ministry recently received 15 acres of land as a donation from the Tribble Foundation about a mile from their house. The Rackleys hope to establish two additional cottages, each housing eight-10 children with houseparents. This time, the entire community will be actively involved from the beginning.

The Rackleys have given up much for the children. Several years back, Anne had secretly saved to buy Joe a king-sized bed as an anniversary gift. Joe had always wanted one.

Shortly after purchasing the bed, the Rackleys moved to a mobile home behind the house so that the newly hired houseparents could sleep in his new king-sized bed. Joe took it all in stride and didn't complain about the change in arrangements because he knew it was good for the future of the ministry.

Now getting older, Joe and Anne don't know if they can keep their present pace up forever, but it's clear that they will always have their hearts devoted to their Collins Kids and perpetuating the ministry.

Mama Anne and Daddy Joe are everyday people who have chosen to sacrifice their personal lives and answer a calling to serve children in need.

"You love the ones who are easy to love, but you also have to love the ones who are not so easy to love," Anne said. "All children have potential and desire the opportunity to lead worthwhile lives."

"I care about people. Even deaf children were helped by the Multi-Board concept because they were able to communicate with it."

- Warren Detrick on the benefits of his creation

DAY 3
Only in America

Happiness. Love. Inspiration. Enthusiasm. They certainly have been here this evening. All are well deserved.

As we have all seen on the basketball courts and on television, the true meaning of magic is a love of helping - a love for your fellow teammates - and a love of winning.

This all leads to being true champions. Champions in every walk of life as individuals and teams. We wish Earvin Johnson and Greg Kelser much happiness and success in their new venture into the NBA.

All of these exciting opportunities can only happen in the most beautiful country in the world - our America!

And with that, Warren Detrick produced a gigantic American flag and waved it across the stage at the Banquet of Champions as Lansing and East Lansing, Mich., celebrated Michigan State's 1978-79 NCAA basketball championship.

Producing such magic - even for Magic Johnson - has been a forte of Warren's in his nearly 80 years on earth. After all, that's what you expect from the person who created the white marker board with color markers, an innovation that is now standard equipment in offices around the world and which played an important role in the flights of all the Apollo lunar modules built in the U.S. space program. The device has even been a tremendous help in classrooms across America. It has been especially helpful in the education process for deaf children.

Warren created the Multi-Board concept while he was with a company named William Reichenbach in Lansing. Michigan State's legendary football coach, Duffy Daughtery, was Warren's friend and first customer for the Multi-Board.

"Duffy was my friend," Warren said. "I saw him at Ken's Barber Shop in East Lansing getting a haircut. I kidded him and said, 'Last week, if you had our new white board and marked the plays in color, you could have won the Notre Dame game (the famous 10-10 tie between the two top-ranked teams in 1966).'

"I have a small board in my car," Warren continued.

"Go get it," Duffy said.

"When I came back in," Warren said, "Duffy was getting his hair washed. With his head dripping water in the sink, I drew a play with water-color markers and erased it with a cloth.

"Bubba Smith was one of my favorite players at the time, so I said to him, 'Duffy, if Bubba ever misses a block, you can write it and erase it on the projection screen or use magnets; that's the versatile part of this concept.' Duffy told me he liked what he saw and asked if I had a name for the board.

"I told Duffy, no - it was only a week old. He smiled and said, 'Call it Multi-Board.' I told him I'd be in touch."

After that, Warren went back and talked with business associate, Bill Reichenbach, about his meeting with Duffy. Bill told him that if he could get Duffy to sign a release and have a picture taken with him, he would form a new company and call it The Multi-Board Co. He would make a 4-by-6 mobile board on wheels and give it to him.

"I called Duffy back and Sylvia, his secretary, put me right through," Warren recalled, telling the coach he won the contest by naming the new white board.

"Duffy said, 'What did I win?'" Warren replied, "Just $10, coach; we're really poor.' He laughed and told me to give it to charity, but we did make a 4-by-6 board for him.

"Duffy posed with the board for a color photo and signed a release for it. This started the ball rolling."

Warren was sales manager and vice president of Multi-Board Co. in the beginning. He went to Eberhard-Faber in Wilkes-Barre, Pa., because he knew that if he didn't have the correct markers, it wouldn't work.

Warren made a presentation to Mr. Faber and his staff in 1967. Paul Mailloux, a vice president of E-F, gave Warren a two-page letter saying the markers could be made. The executive said E-F would be interested in marketing the new Multi-Board. When Reichenbach saw the letter, he flew back to Wilkes-Barre and Bill offered to sell the company to Eberhard-Faber.

Eberhard-Faber purchased the company and made Warren sales manager of Multi-Board Co., which became a subsidiary of Eberhard-Faber. A new manufacturing plant was built in Lansing in 1967. Later on, Warren created a talking board concept with a wireless microphone in the 1970s. He retired in 1982.

Warren says many people have thought of him as a scientist and engineer, but in fact, he says he has no mechanical aptitude at all. He can read situations and understand people, however.

"I care about people," he says. "I think the thing I'm most proud of with the Multi-Board is that deaf children were helped by the concept."

Warren's development of the Multi-Board didn't come easily. Many people were critical of him personally or skeptical of the commercial potential of his concept.

He recalled one incident with a Michigan State professor. The two of them were talking, and Warren made the mistake of saying the board could eventually eliminate the chalkboard and chalk dust.

The professor looked at Warren and said, "Young man, I've been working for 40 years with these messy chalkboards," he said. "When I go home from work, if I don't have dust on my suit, I don't feel as if I've done my job. The chalk dust is a symbol of who I am. The Multi-Board will never replace the chalkboard."

Warren remembered once having the flu and becoming depressed because he thought the Multi-Board wasn't going to make it. When Warren's daughters, Jenny and Julie, encouraged him not to give up, he persevered, and the board became a national, then international success.

One of Warren's favorite quotes is "THE COURAGE TO RISK FAILURE LEADS TO SUCCESS."

Warren has spent most of his life trying to enhance the communication process. When he was doubted after developing the revolutionary Multi-Board concept, he did not give up. Even in retirement, Warren and his wife, Ellie, have done what they could to help disadvantaged children and others who need their help.

One Saturday, I was driving through Warren's neighborhood in Seneca, S.C., and saw a sign that read, "Collins Children's Home - Newspaper Drive, Saturday, 13033 Azalea Drive." I wanted to find out more so I stopped and chatted with Warren and Ellie.

I learned that each month for the last eight years, Warren and Ellie have held a recycling paper drive in their garage for the Collins Home.

"We average about three trunk fulls of paper each month that we take to the Collins Home," said Warren. "The recycling effort is about 12 percent of their annual support."

Warren loves children. After he developed the Multi-Board, Warren became a magician and has done countless shows for children, but never charged a dime.

Today, the Multi-Board concept is found all over the world, in conference rooms like those at the World Trade Center in New York and the Sears Tower in Chicago, newsrooms, hospitals, schools and all sorts of businesses. It's also used at golf tournaments, basketball games, seminars and countless other gatherings to illustrate points, diagram plays, keep track of times and has many other useful purposes. The Multi-Board still assists the deaf in classroom communication. Today, the white board is even interfaced with computers.

"I do want to pay tribute to Walt Krieger, vice president of marketing at Eberhard-Faber," Warren said. "He was my close friend and greatest supporter during the 16 years of marketing this concept. Unfortunately, I lost this valued friendship when Walt passed away in November 1993.

"It makes me feel very good to have pioneered the concept. I'm not a wealthy man, but I'm wealthy in my heart because I'm helping people communicate in all walks of life."

Warren is a man who changed the way the world communicates with his Multi-Board, but hasn't forgotten to do simple things like free magic and antique toy shows for children, Saturday paper drives or soliciting new subscribers free of charge to the local newspaper.

"Donna has taught me a lot by being kind, gentle, loving and understanding. She is just a marvelous person, very thoughtful."

- Marcelle Gustavel on her daughter, Donna, who has cerebral palsy

DAY 4
The Courage to Live

Each step in Donna Gustavel's life has required more courage than most of us could possibly imagine.

Because of cerebral palsy (a disease which affects the central nervous system), Donna wasn't even able to take her first steps until she was 5 years old.

Donna, who lives in Keowee Key, S.C., could have had a normal life if a condition she had at birth had been diagnosed properly. Donna had a Rh blood factor when she was born and should have had her blood immediately exchanged, but doctors waited too long to do so. Her blood was eventually exchanged, but by the time it happened, it was too late; the damage had already been done.

Not only did Donna develop palsy, she was also born deaf, and she wasn't expected to live past her 20th birthday. But Donna Gustavel, now 41, has more than doubled that prognosis.

"They told me that if she made it to 21, it would be wonderful," Marcelle told me. "She is an incredible person and is still going strong. She's as sharp as a tack."

Marcelle said that Donna would have never walked had it not been for her strong will and an occupational and physical therapist who believed in her.

"Everything has been harder for her than for normal people," Marcelle said. "She had to be taught how to do everything, from sitting, walking, even tying her shoelaces. Once she learned how to walk, she tip-toed so fast, I couldn't keep up with her."

I had met Donna before, but one day, I had the pleasure of sitting down with Donna, her father, Don, and Ed Rumsey, owner of the Kourthouse Fitness Center in Keowee Key. I soon learned that Donna has been a blessing in the eyes of Don and her mother, Marcelle.

"Donna has taught me a lot by being kind, gentle, loving and understanding," Marcelle told me. "She is just a marvelous person; very thoughtful."

Cerebral palsy and deafness aren't the only things Donna has had to endure; during her life, she has suffered numerous internal problems, two or three melograms, three fusions of the cervical vertebrae in her back and having to have her sixth and seventh vertebrae bracketed and wired together.

Yet, through all that, she has remained tougher than most people in her situation could even imagine and always kept a positive attitude on life.

"She is tough as nails," Rumsey told me. He was so taken with Donna and became so close, he even learned sign language so he could speak to her. "If you're looking for anyone with more guts and courage in Oconee County, I think it would very difficult to find."

Donna came with her parents to Keowee Key after her dad, Don, retired as an Atlanta executive and she retired as a teacher's assistant in the DeKalb County, Ga., schools in the mid-1980s. Donna makes it a point to work out, despite what must be constant pain, by getting on the Stairmaster and treadmill nearly every day.

Rumsey said seeing Donna Gustavel on the treadmill or Stairmaster, moving her twisted body around on those machines, while others complain about a sore knee, or some other minor ailment, really drives home what determination and guts is all about.

One time, I saw her take an incredible fall to the floor. I started to walk over to help, but before I could get there, she was already back on her feet and on the Stairmaster.

"She always picks herself up from whatever she is doing when she falls," Marcelle told me. "One time, she took a terrible fall, with the impact on the side of her face, and it knocked her glasses off. I was very upset when she didn't get up right away, but she raised her hands to signal she was all right. That calmed me down."

Donna has been battling the odds all her life with her multiple handicaps. Once, when she was a student, a school refused to accept her because of her handicaps. Another time, a bus driver didn't want to let her on the bus because he thought she would be a hardship.

Donna has an unbelievably kind heart, which has remained despite the obstacles. "She's been such an inspiration to me, her father and the rest of her family," Marcelle said. "She's also inspired many others with her warmth and love for other people.

"She is such a giving person. She would have made a wonderful teacher," her neurologist said, "if she hadn't had cerebral palsy. She has a wonderful mind. She wanted to get A's in school, period!"

Donna stays busy with her pet Chihuahua named Luv, helps with household chores and occasionally makes a special batch of chocolate chip cookies, which draws raves around Keowee Key. She also has an insatiable craving for Coca-Cola's pioneering diet cola, Tab. Her father often makes special trips to Atlanta, Coke's home city, just to get the soda she loves.

She has a very special friend in one of the greatest golfers of all time, Jack Nicklaus, whom the Gustavels met in Reynolds Plantation, S.C., where they each own property. "The Golden Bear" took some time to write to Donna after reading my column about her life, saying he agreed with everything I had written about her "wholeheartedly!" Nicklaus, too, loves Donna's chocolate chip cookies and frequently writes to her.

She is also buddies with singer Tony Bennett, whom Marcelle has known since their childhood days in Long Island, N.Y. Once, when Bennett performed at the Peace Center in Greenville, S.C., he dedicated two of the songs to Donna and sang them directly to her, which became one of her lifetime thrills.

Courage is a sometimes overused word, but in Donna Gustavel's case, courage doesn't even begin to describe what she has inside.

Just being around her is inspiration enough.

Dear Donna:

Thanks for your nice note and the copy of Dan Brannan's great article. I enjoyed it a lot and agree with him wholeheartedly.

It has been a while since our paths have crossed, but I am happy to know you are doing well - and still making those chocolate chip cookies.

Say hello to your parents for me, and keep up all the good work at the gym.

Your friend,

Jack Nicklaus

"If there is something you want to do, and you make up your mind, you can do it. Don't be limited by someone else's expectations for yourself."

- Tony Sample on his philosophy of overcoming limitations with having only one functional arm

DAY 5
An Inspiring Best Friend

The Bethalto, Ill., bowling center had fallen silent on this cold March 12, 1992, Midwestern night.

All eyes were focused on a 6-foot-5, 200-pound bowler closing in on his first perfect game.

Tony Sample, a 32-year-old Roodhouse, Ill., resident, had just rolled eight consecutive strikes.

"There were a lot of people watching," said Tony. "That's what usually happens if someone is close to bowling a 300 game."

This was not the first time Tony had been under pressure and come through. In fact, since birth, he had been beating the odds, defying the fact that he was born with only one perfectly functional arm.

Tony was a breech baby, coming out feet first. Because of strain on his right shoulder, the muscles and nerves were damaged and never fully developed.

Tony said he felt numb after completing his eighth strike on that March evening.

"I got extra nervous and didn't have much self-awareness," he said. "I had never been able to throw that 11th or 12th strike for a 300 game.

"But when I let loose of my last ball for the 300 game, I felt I made about as good a shot as I could."

The 16-pound object rolled down the 60-foot lane to the head pin and...

The ball smashed the pins! Tony had his first 300 game as a bowler.

Three weeks later, on April 2, Tony was back in the spotlight at the same center, closing in on a 300 game again.

"I was much more in control that night," Tony said. "I was still nervous after the 10th frame, but I knew I had been able to throw it once."

Tony kept his composure and did it again, rolling another 300 game.

A year later, Tony took part in his first Professional Bowlers Association tour event in Collinsville, Ill. He said taking part in a PBA event was the fulfillment of a long-time aspiration.

For years, I had been watching Tony with the utmost respect and sometimes amazement. I was there the day he took part in the PBA event; in fact, I sponsored him.

I was so proud of him that day because he had worked so hard to get there.

Tony and I met in kindergarten at Carrollton Elementary School. We have been friends ever since.

I can't imagine how difficult it was for Tony to become so skilled at hitting, catching and throwing a baseball. We played on the same teams every year during the summer baseball leagues. Tony was the first baseman; I played second base. On the basketball court, we both played forward.

Tony and I played nearly every sport together during our childhood years. During football season, we played football at either my house or his house two blocks away on Maple Street. The same held true for basketball, baseball, boxing, hockey or whatever sport was in season.

Tony's left arm was extremely strong. One time, when we were boxing, he pounded me in the face about six straight times and I thought I had been hit with a sledgehammer. I also remember the two of us putting up a hockey goal in front of his house in the middle of the street and playing one-on-one hockey. We would fire at the goal for hours, pretending we were Red Berenson and Garry Unger, two of our heroes at the time with the St. Louis Blues hockey team.

I was fortunate enough to have played football at school, but Tony was not; the doctors felt that playing football would pose too much of a risk of injury to his other arm.

I think he could have been a tremendous football player. In fact, when we were kids, I remember Tony placed first once and second three other times in the now-defunct Ford NFL Punt, Pass and Kick competition one year (a competition since revived and sponsored by Gatorade).

When I was 9, Tony went to Denver to see a specialist. While Tony was in Colorado, all his team members kneeled down at their bedsides and said prayers that he would return with an arm as good as new. I took over at first base while Tony was gone and absolutely hated playing without him.

"I had been seeing a chiropractor in Carrollton and he felt if anything could be done for my right arm, Denver was the place for me to go," said Tony. "I didn't go with any expectations, so I wasn't disappointed when nothing could be done."

When Tony came back from Denver and told us the news, we all felt bad. We thought at the time our prayers had not been answered.

Tony shrugged it off and kept practicing. His folks moved across town to a new house and built him a basketball court. Hour upon hour, he shot baskets. When he wasn't shooting baskets, he was playing catch, hitting a baseball or cracking the books to keep up on his studies.

"Every time I played catch, I practiced taking the glove on and off, so I guess that's why I got pretty good at it," said Tony.

When he caught the ball the glove had to come off for him to throw. Tony could take that glove off so fast, much like baseball pitcher Jim Abbott, it would make your head spin.

By the time we were in high school, Tony had become an accomplished athlete.

One night Carrollton High was playing Auburn High. When Coach Steve Dunn barked out the starting lineup, Tony's name was included in the group of five.

"I hadn't been playing much and when he said I was starting, I said, 'Yeah, right.' I went out and made everything I shot," Tony said, after finishing the game with 22 points. Later in the season, he scored 23 points against North Greene. Our team finished the year 16-0.

During his senior season, Tony batted .415 on the baseball team. For years, his license plates read "TS 415."

Tony was absolutely incredible at the plate his senior year. It seemed every time he batted, he got a base hit; it was the second-best average in the entire St. Louis area.

"I just wanted to see the ball, hit it squarely and get the ball in play between the foul lines in right or left field," he said. "I wanted to see the ball and put the bat on it."

With two completely functional arms, I think Tony would have played professional baseball. Tony laughs when I say that.

Tony wasn't just an outstanding athlete. He had a brilliant mind and was an exceptional student, earning an Illinois State Scholarship for his academic excellence.

Eventually, Tony became a partner in a family insurance business in Roodhouse. Tony and his beautiful wife, Charlene, have two children - Yvonne, 11, and Alicia, 9.

Today, Tony devotes much of his free time to his adorable girls, participating in their school functions in various activities. Tony is as persistent at being a good husband and father as he was swinging a bat or swishing a corner jump shot.

I've known many inspirations in my life, but I doubt if many could compare to Tony. I watched him evolve from the time he was 6 into what he is today. Tony always had to work harder than the rest of us. Nothing came easy for him.

Tony wasn't defensive about his arm; in fact, he always was the class comic and kept things light and relaxing with his sense of humor. When I needed to talk, there wasn't a better listener than Tony.

We never talked much about his dysfunctional arm when we were growing up.

Nearly 30 years after we first met, I asked him, "What motivated you to become as accomplished as you are?" I could picture him grinning even though we were conversing on the phone and 600 miles apart.

"I wanted to play on the first team and didn't want to sit on the bench or play intramurals," he laughed with his ever-present humor.

I then asked him, "Tony, if you had to give a boy or girl with a similar obstacle a piece of advice, what would it be?"

"I'd say if there is something you want to do and you make up your mind; you can do it," Tony said. "Don't be limited by someone else's expectations for yourself."

DAY 6

The Civil War's Final Shot

═══════════

When he was just 20 years old, Joe Stokley seemed to have the world at his feet.

He had already sailed through his course requirements at the University of Florida in Gainesville, and just lacked the student teaching requirement before completing his bachelor's degree in education. He had always wanted to be a teacher.

The date was Feb. 1, 1958. He was visiting relatives in Baltimore when the unthinkable happened.

While playing the piano, Stokley didn't notice a young cousin who had an old Civil War-era muzzle loader in his hands, just 18 inches away.

The cousin had been playing with the gun in recent days, firing caps inside of it. He had just loaded about 10 caps into the side hammer of the 10-gauge muzzle loader before he pointed it at Stokley's face. The relic had not been used since the Civil War and would have been last loaded with shot and powder during that time frame in the 1860s.

Stokley doesn't remember what happened; he only knows what other relatives told him about the incident.

"It sounded like a cannon going off," Stokley's father told him.

About a pound of shot passed through Stokley on one side of his face and went out the other, taking his tongue, large portions of jawbone and several teeth in the process.

After passing through Stokley, the blast just missed the young cousin's mother, who just previously had been sitting on a sofa which was hit as well, and shattering the window above it. Stokley's grandfather, singing with the piano, was hit in the neck and shoulder during the incident.

Stokley collapsed to the floor after the shooting. His grandfather lunged for him and desperately strained to hold him upright so he would not drown in his own blood.

During the rough ambulance ride to the hospital, Stokley's aunt, who was a nurse, held what remained of his jaw in place, although it was shattered. Hospital officials later told Stokley without that particular assistance, the outcome might well have been fatal.

Stokley was rushed to Johns Hopkins University Hospital in Baltimore following the incident. His father said the ride to the hospital was the most harrowing of his entire life.

"The ambulance made eight miles in eight minutes through city traffic, and the roads were covered with snow and ice that day," Stokley said his father told him.

"If the shot had entered a few millimeters higher in any other direction, it would have killed me instantly," Stokley said. "If my cousin had been any closer or any farther back, I would have been killed. I was very lucky that day."

Some may not have viewed him as lucky. His mouth was wired shut for months, and he could not even talk for nearly a year. As his rehabilitation went on, his progress was measured in small increments every day.

Stokley didn't even learn exactly what happened to him until a nurse showed him a copy of an article about the incident in the Sunday *Baltimore Sun* on the Tuesday following the accident.

Hospital personnel doubted if Stokley would ever speak again, but he didn't listen to them. He learned to say his alphabet - without a tongue - practicing for hours each day.

Next came words, then sentences. He had several operations during his recovery period. Stokley had four operations on his jaw at Johns Hopkins in February 1958, then two additional surgeries the following summer involving bone grafts. Later in New Orleans, he had four additional skin grafts and facial reconstruction.

Stokley said the one brief time that he lost the will to live was after an all-day procedure in the summer of 1958.

"I was in so much pain and nausea that I felt I would rather die," he said. "I had been under anesthesia during a nine-hour operation for a bone graft to the lower jaw. That was an extremely long time back then."

Miraculously, about a year later, in February 1959, Stokley persuaded one of his former teachers to supervise his student teaching so he could complete his bachelor's of science degree. His face was still disfigured, and he looked extremely odd. He was hard to understand verbally, but nevertheless, he taught every day and finished his requirement to become a certified mathematics teacher.

Stokley began his career as a substitute teacher at a Florida high school. He was offered a full-time position in November 1959 when the person for which he was substituting failed to return to school. It was the break he had been waiting for. Stokley had became a full-fledged teacher despite all that had happened to him.

"I had made so much progress by this point," Stokley said. "It was a challenge every day. It was tough working with teen-agers. They had to adjust to me. Once people got to know my situation, they were very helpful. I had very active relationships in my church. I had support at every turn. No one ever gave me a hard time about anything."

Stokley continued to teach in public schools in Florida, Maryland and Virginia. He also worked as an industrial engineer at a chemical plant in Virginia for three years. Stokley received his master's degree from Longwood College in Farmville, Va., and did graduate work at the University of Wyoming in Laramie, Wyo. In 1972, he received a permanent teaching position at North Greenville College in Greenville, S.C.

Marriage was not something constantly on Stokley's mind in the months that initially followed the accident.

"I was struggling to survive," said Stokley. "I didn't have much of a social life. I didn't spend much time meeting new people; I was trying to make progress."

Joe met the woman who would become his wife, Sue Edmonds, through mutual family friends. Joe and Sue were married in June 1966 and had four lovely children.

"It has been very fulfilling having children," said Joe. "I feel very fortunate to have had four children. I believe anyone who is able to have children receives quite a blessing."

Today, it's not even evident that Joe has no tongue, and a beard covers up the scars his face still bears.

Joe does not consider his personal trials and tribulations much different from anyone else's struggles.

"I think there are junctures in everyone's life where there are crises and setbacks," he said. "I spent a lot of time in prayer and focused on what happened to me. A situation like that can be an opportunity to look at your life and ask the Lord what he would have you do."

The incident reinforced the importance of a passage in the Biblical book of Romans, which reads, *"And we know that in all things God works for the good of those who love him, and who have been called according to his purpose."* (Romans 8:28)

"This passage gives you the philosophy to cope with setbacks," said Joe.

"I don't know what I would have done if it hadn't been for the support of friends and family and their prayers," he said. "There wasn't a day that went by that I didn't get a letter or a personal visit from someone after I got shot. I personally believe everyone has a Guardian Angel; it all depends on how receptive you are of the Holy Spirit. God never gives you more than you can bear."

"I didn't want to be a blind man with the stereotype of holding a cane and selling pencils."

- Matthew Phillips on why he worked so hard to get his college degree

DAY 7
So What's a Little Blindness?

Inspirations come in many shapes, sizes and forms.

Twenty-eight-year old Matthew Phillips is one such example.

Phillips, who resides in Seneca, S.C., didn't let total blindness stop him from completing the requirements at Clemson University for a bachelor's degree in sociology.

He told me that walking up on the platform at Clemson's Littlejohn Coliseum during the December 1995 graduation ceremonies was the proudest moment of his life.

"It was a very proud moment for my family," he said.

Phillips was born three months premature, weighing in at only a pound and a half. "I was so small, I had to be put in an incubator, and they gave me too much oxygen," he told me. "That caused me to go blind.

"Today, I feel just as normal as anyone else. I've gone through the public school system all my life. I have no regrets about being blind."

Phillips started his post-high school trek at Central Wesleyan College in Central, S.C. (the school is now known as Southern Wesleyan University) soon after his graduation from Seneca High School. He majored in music, but left several years later, enrolling at Tri-County Technical College in Pendleton, S.C., then transferring to Clemson in the fall of 1991. It took him a while to decide on his major, but eventually he decided on sociology.

Being blind and going to school presented some unique challenges to Phillips. He used several techniques to study, such as records for the blind, Braille text and readers.

In fact, he often asked friends of his to read textbooks for him on tape. Many of the other readers were members of the Lions Club, who typically donate much time and energy to assist the blind.

"I have purchased a lot of books at the bookstore and hired people to read them on tape," he said. "There were also members of the Salem (S.C.) Lions Club who read on some of those tapes. Whether or not I had more than one reading on a tape depended on how much material I had to do. If there were two books in a course, I would have two people read on the tapes to me.

"Back when I was going to Central Wesleyan College, there were times I would rely on fellow students coming to read to me, and they wouldn't show up. Sometimes, I would be desperate for someone to read to me so I could study for my classes. I could always count on the Salem Lions Club. I probably would not have gotten through college without their help."

In his later college years, Phillips used a computer with a scanner that reads material with a speech synthesizer, part of a technological revolution that has helped the blind immensely. "It's amazing what has been done to help blind people," Phillips said. "Having this synthesizer really helped me a lot."

Phillips doesn't believe what he did was anything ultra-spectacular. "You just have to work a little harder if you are blind," he said.

He was always determined that his blindness would not slow him down. "I didn't want to be a blind man with the stereotype of holding a cane and selling pencils," he said. "I always knew I would get my college degree; I just had to find my niche.

"I always wanted to be an independent person."

Matthew is the son of Betty Phillips of Seneca, and she has always been very supportive of him and made him stand on his own two feet.

"I remember one time when I was 7 years old and I was getting ready to go on a trip for the blind to Nags Head, N.C.," Matthew said. "I was scared, but my mother took me to Greenville and made me get on the bus. My parents always wanted me to be like everyone else."

Matt's mom, Betty, always pushed him to do the things normal children did. "I had ideas of how I wanted to raise my children," she said. "Matt was blind, and I didn't know exactly what to do, but I had a mental image of what I hoped he would become. I constantly made him do things he was afraid of.

"One time, I carried him to the barber shop when he didn't want to go. I calmed him down and convinced him to go ahead with the haircut. After that, he was OK. Another time, he was afraid to swing on a swing set, but I went ahead and told him to do it. After he did it, he didn't have any problems with the swing set.

"I'm very proud of all the things he's done."

One of the few regrets Matthew ever had was not being able to get his driver's license at age 16. "It was hard for me when all my friends got their licenses," he said.

Despite that, Matthew has nothing but positive thoughts about his future. He plans to enroll in graduate school at Clemson University and obtain his master's degree in psychology, focusing on community agency counseling.

"I want to do what I can to counsel and help people with disabilities, not just the visually impaired," he said. "I would like to work with people who have substance-abuse problems and work with dysfunctional families."

Matthew says many blind people have attitude problems once they become blind. With a slight attitude adjustment, it is unbelievable what a person who can't see can accomplish.

"Brian is physically and mentally challenged, but it has never slowed him down. If there was ever an angel on earth, Brian is one. He's my own private little angel..."

- Benita Griffin on her brother, Brian Compton

DAY 8
An Angel on Earth

Brian Keith Compton's story is one that involves not only his individual battle to survive as a mentally and physically challenged person, but how he served as the catalyst for the family around him to grow and learn the appreciation of family and what is most important in life.

Brian was born with multiple birth defects.

Brian's father, Al Compton, was in the U.S. Air Force, serving as a technical sergeant, when Brian was born March 17, 1967, at Sasebo Naval Hospital in Japan. Al was in the middle of a three-year tour of duty in Japan when Brian was born.

"We were limited at the naval hospital in pediatric care," Al said. "I had to make a choice of what I was going to do with my enlistment. I was approaching my 17th year in the service."

Al encountered difficulties in getting the right kind of transfer so Brian could get the proper medical care. After going back and forth with The Pentagon, he had 30 days left before his discharge.

Compton made the decision to return to the United States and give up 18 years in the military for his son and family. Al Compton was only two years away from full military retirement.

"I was only making $524 a month as a technical sergeant," Al said. "The first thing I did when I got back was file for a civil service commission."

Brian, who is a mentally and physically challenged adult, doesn't seek recognition for the things he does. But because of all the ways he helps people, Brian found himself selected by Spartanburg, S.C., CBS affiliate WSPA-TV as its "Hero of the Day," a daily feature during morning newscasts.

He described his selection as the biggest thrill of his life. "It was great," Brian said of his honor. "It is definitely one of my proudest moments.

"This is the first time something like this has happened to me."

Brian was nominated by his sister, Benita Griffin. In her letter of nomination, Griffin said, "Brian is physically and mentally challenged, but it has never slowed him down. Brian volunteers at the local hospital and has worked there for three years. He never misses a day, even though he's never paid a dime. Brian is very involved with his church.

"He writes songs and plays which he performs for the church whenever he is able. If there was ever an angel on earth, Brian is one. He's my own private little angel, and I guess I am biased because I'm his big sister. It was great he was picked for this honor."

Brian is part of an American Red Cross team which volunteers its services at Oconee Memorial Hospital in Seneca. His duties are many and varied.

"I answer the phone, pick up patients and pick up flowers that go to the room," he said. "I have done this for about the last several years. I think it is the thing to do.

"I work from 4:30-8 p.m. Wednesdays and from 2:30-8 p.m. Saturdays."

Tina Kirby, another one of Brian's sisters, says her brother is precious.

"He's never done anything ugly to anybody," said Kirby. "I think he keeps my dad, Al, alive. My dad was very close to retiring with a pension in the service, but he gave it up to be with Brian. Dad would have re-enlisted if the military would have flown our family to South Carolina, where our mother and father's family were.

"After Brian was born, the military gave Dad a chance to go overseas again, but they were only willing to fly his family from Japan, where Brian was born, to California. We had six children to take care of, and my parent's family would have helped us.

"He requested that the family be allowed to fly to South Carolina. They refused. They would, however, *have* to pay for the entire family to return to South Carolina if Al were to decline to re-enlist.

"He chose not to re-enlist to ensure that he and his family were together in South Carolina so that Brian could get the needed medical help and support. He was only a year and a half away from getting his military pension, and he lost everything when he decided not to re-enlist. Today, my dad spends every day with him."

After stints in Baltimore and Atlanta, Al moved his family back to Seneca in February 1969. Brian then began the process of seeing specialized pediatric care in Columbia, S.C., in an attempt to correct his birth defects. The problem with his heart was eliminated, then they worked on his feet with braces; he had to visit the specialist for several years.

During the first three years of his life, Brian's family were the only ones who could understand him. When it was time for him to begin kindergarten, children with any mental or physical disabilities could not enroll in the public school system. Al continued to battle for his son and eventually, Brian enrolled in first grade.

Once Brian graduated from high school, he obtained a job with the Bi-Lo supermarket in Seneca and did very well. He also worked at J.P. Stevens (now WestPoint Stevens). Al describes Brian as a dependable, hard worker.

When Brian was named as Hero of the Day, Al said it was a very big moment for the entire family. "Brian does a lot of wonderful things with his church and other people," Al said. "He is very sociable."

Kirby added that Brian has very strong Christian beliefs and does look at things from a child's viewpoint.

"All he knows is to love other people," said Kirby.

Brian graduated from Seneca High School in 1986 in the regular curriculum, then attended Tri-County Technical College in Pendleton, S.C. He has also been a delivery person for the *Journal/Tribune* newspaper in Seneca.

Al said Brian has made a tremendous difference in his life. "He gives me something to live for each day," Al said.

Brian is a person who believes he needs to give back what he has received. "A lot of people have helped me through the years, so I guess this is my way of giving back," he said.

Brian is a person who has not forgotten the Biblical saying, "Those who give shall receive."

DAY 9

When Worlds Collide

Ashley McCoy, a Seneca (S.C.) High School freshman, and Jake Einhorn, a vice president at the prestigious New York clothing store Saks Fifth Avenue, were on completely different paths in The Big Apple one day.

All of a sudden, because of some incredible circumstances, their worlds collided.

McCoy was on a school trip to New York with her history class when, unknown to her, she dropped her wallet.

At the same time, Einhorn was busy with Spring Fashion Week shows on Seventh Avenue in Manhattan when he found McCoy's wallet.

"We discovered her wallet on a bus," Einhorn said. "It had been a very busy week here in New York. We were attending Matsuda shows, and they provided complementary bus service.

"At first, our fashion director had found her wallet, and he said it had an ID of a child inside it. I asked our director if he wanted to take care of it or if he wanted me to take care of it, and we decided that I would take care of this. I immediately put the wallet in my coat."

At that time, McCoy was already upset after learning her wallet was gone. It contained $289, a large sum of money for a 14-year-old girl.

"I was terribly upset," she recalled. "I thought I had lost it in the street while we were unpacking baggage. My teacher, Glen Abbott, and chaperone, Margaret Rich, helped me a lot by loaning me money for food and souvenirs."

When Einhorn returned to his office, he counted the money and realized that there must be one upset South Carolina girl out in the bustling Manhattan streets. "I felt badly for the girl," Einhorn said. "I knew she must have been to New York on a trip, and I knew to lose that kind of money would be devastating for someone that age.

"Once, when I was a kid, I lost 50 cents on the way home from the five-and-dime after buying some crayons. I never forgot how upset I was about that. I thought of this girl coming to New York and losing her wallet.

"New York is a great city; I guess I just wanted her to have good memories about being in New York."

A few days later, Einhorn called Seneca High School and asked if he should write a check for the cash in the wallet. He then returned the wallet and ID completely intact.

"It's incredible what Jake Einhorn did," said Abbott. "From his actions, I think the children learned that people are people, no matter where they go.

"It's a culture shock coming from Seneca to a city like New York. They had heard New Yorkers are rude, but this incident has shown them otherwise. This was a very positive thing to happen to us. I can't imagine many people finding a wallet like this and returning it. This should strengthen Ashley's faith in humanity."

A few days later, Ashley received a letter from Einhorn, which said:

Dear Ashley:

Attached you will find a check in the amount of $289.00, along with your wallet and ID card. My secretary informed me that you were in New York on a school trip. It was most unfortunate for you to lose your wallet, but I hope this return restores your faith in New Yorkers.

" I've made several trips with students to New York," Abbott said, "but I think this is the most special of the trips we've made because of this incident.

"I couldn't believe it when the school secretary, Anita Hart, told me we got a phone call at 4 in the afternoon that Monday from Jake Einhorn's office in New York. Her eyes were gleaming when she told me about it."

Those who believe busy corporate executives can't perform good deeds may now think twice after hearing about McCoy's story.

Einhorn is a nationally known fashion executive, but also believes that each good deed a person does can make a big difference over time.

"My creed in life is that any good deed does make a difference," he said. "This is the second time I've found a wallet like this. The first time it had $120 and a bank card in it. I called the person's bank and told them to contact the person and tell him I had the wallet. I never heard from anyone. The wallet sat in my desk for more than two years without anyone calling about it. I'm just glad I was able to return everything to the girl in South Carolina."

McCoy told me the experience has changed her outlook on New Yorkers and big corporate executives.

"I feel like there are honest people in New York City," McCoy told me. "I didn't really know this could be true, but now, I do."

"I called Converse College and asked if there was an age limit for their students. When I told them how old I was, I don't think they knew exactly what to say. It's kept my mind fresh, having this type of hobby."

- 83-year-old beginning violin player, Evelyn Coggins

DAY 10
Life Begins at 80

Many people have lifelong dreams that are, unfortunately, never realized. Evelyn Coggins of Spartanburg, S.C., was almost one of those people.

She had a lifelong dream to play the violin, but as a girl growing up in Spartanburg, there were no violin teachers and no orchestra programs in public schools. Plus, she had too many chores to perform at home when she got back from school. Music lessons were a luxury that no one could afford.

Evelyn was always busy with her two children and her husband, Fred, until he died in 1983.

In the back of her mind, Evelyn always wanted to play beautiful music on the violin. The dream began when she was in fourth grade and it never really faded. But, her husband had Alzheimer's disease in the final years of his life, and as she said, "It was a terrible thing to go through. I needed something to hold on to, something to occupy my time."

That's when the longing to play the violin resurfaced in her life.

"I called Converse College (she was in her late 70s at the time) and asked if there was an age limit for their students," she said. "When I told them how old I was, I don't think they exactly knew what to say."

She studied her first year under Dean Curry, and in that first year, the process was a slow one.

"I didn't think I was progressing very well," she recalled. "I kept trying and studied very hard. I still had the desire to learn.

"The next year, I had a new teacher, Peter Moore, and he has been very good to me. He explained and showed me what I needed to do to improve."

She now has lessons once a week and continues to show improvement.

Evelyn is the oldest pupil Moore has taught. "I've known some people that were near their 70s when they started, but she started at 79," Moore said. "The violin has given new meaning to her life. She's not the type of person who can sit around and watch soap operas all day. She's very serious about practicing for even several hours a day.

"She plays recitals and sometimes plays in church. The violin has become the central focus of her existence. She now owns several violins.

"It's been a wonderful feeling working with her. I sometimes teach young people who are coming to lessons because their parents want them to; they don't take it very seriously. Mrs. Coggins takes notes on everything I say and is very critical of herself. She has inspired me. I now see that people can do anything at any age if they put their minds to it.

"She is also always baking me treats. She has become like a family member to me. We are very good friends."

What makes it even more of a struggle to practice or perform is her battle with a heart problem; she even has a pacemaker installed in her body.

Moore vividly recalls his first encounter with Coggins. "I only had the list of names of my students," he said. "She walked in. Since the students usually come with their parents, I thought she was waiting for her granddaughter.

"I said, 'Is your daughter or granddaughter coming?' She told me "no," that *she* was the student.

"When the grades were sent out for the first semester, they were addressed to her parents. I had to explain to the office that she didn't have any parents who were still alive!"

Moore usually gives his students half-hour lessons, but he allows 70 minutes for her lessons. "It's not the normal violin lesson," he said. "We spend a lot of time socializing, and I let her rest when she needs to. I know her whole family. She always has to tell me about her great-nephew and what he is doing."

Coggins has established somewhat of a following in the Upstate of South Carolina, with many friends and fans attending her concerts and recitals.

On May 16, 1996, Evelyn turned 84. "I practice every day and sometimes twice a day," she says. "I always wanted to play hymns in church someday. I am a shy person, and so when my son asked me to play in Gaffney (S.C.) at his church, I didn't know if I was good enough to play, but I went anyway.

"I was anxious, but I did OK. I didn't look out to see anybody while I was playing. I guess I just want to continue to get better and better at playing the violin. It's kept my mind fresh, having this type of hobby."

Some would say that 80 years of age is too old to accomplish much of anything; others say life begins at 80.

Evelyn Coggins, at age 84, is certainly a prime example of not letting one's age get in the way of one's dreams.

"We felt beyond a shadow of a doubt that this is what the Lord wanted us to do. You can't believe someone would leave something so beautiful and valuable to die. Out of all the babies left by the side of the river, you became ours."

- Jan Davidson about the adoption of daughter, Anna Marie

DAY 11
Running Through Walls

On June 15, 1995, in a part of the world far from American soil, a newborn baby girl was placed in a plastic bowl by the banks of a river. With the umbilical cord and the afterbirth still attached and blood covering her body, she was destined to be put to a forever sleep by the impending tide.

Back in America, a couple was just beginning to act on their desire to give an unwanted foreign child a chance for a new life filled with love.

Three months later, a series of events which could only be called miraculous caused that infant to be the much-wanted child of Mark and Jan Davidson.

She was named Anna Marie, and her adoption is the result of what many people said couldn't be done.

Not only is she the first baby to be adopted from the deep jungles of Doc Von, Vietnam, but she was adopted without the assistance of paid adoption agencies - not even those specializing in international adoptions.

What Anna Marie Davidson represents, instead, is one couple's gutsy determination to follow their heart, regardless of the odds.

The Davidsons have a biological daughter named Hope, but the couple was sympathetic to the plight of children in international orphanages who have been, as Jan says, "doomed to a life without parents. Both of us decided to have a child of our own, but after one, we would adopt a child from overseas."

The couple had traveled on religious missions in the past and had first-hand knowledge of the conditions present in Third World nations.

It wasn't enough to stop them.

"We knew it didn't matter how much money we had or what material things we had to offer the children as long as we loved them; it would be better than the conditions they were in," Jan said.

At first, the Davidsons had considered adopting a child from a Russian or Romanian orphanage, but Jan was friends with Annie Truong, a Vietnamese native who owned a shop where Jan had her nails done. Annie told the Davidsons that Vietnamese orphanages were in desperate straits, packed to the rafters with newborn infants and operating under primitive - to say the least - conditions.

It was hard for the Davidsons to believe what they were being told about the conditions in Vietnam and, conversely, how easy it was to adopt a child. "But the more I talked to her, the more I began to believe," Jan said.

A year after that conversation, the Davidsons began to put the adoption wheels into motion. They called the U.S. Immigration and Naturalization Service's regional office in Atlanta - and all they got was a computer voice. They spent three weeks trying to get the information they needed before calling the INS office in Washington. By that time, they had become angry, frustrated and disillusioned.

Jan spoke with the U.S. director for overseas adoptions, who called Pam Copeland, the director of the Atlanta office, and instructed her to make the Davidsons her top priority.

Before contacting the government, however, they had spoken to several agencies specializing in international adoptions - and learned they charged anywhere from $18-24,000 for a process that lasted nearly two years. Even adoption officials they had befriended advised them not to go forward on their own; one said the rules changed every day for adoptions.

The process was emotionally and physically draining on the couple, but Jan and Mark were both determined to press on, regardless of the odds, the hardships or the complications.

"We felt beyond the shadow of a doubt that this was what the Lord wanted us to do," Jan said.

The INS eventually approved the Davidsons for an adoption. With the help of Annie, Jan and Mark filled out the paperwork required by the Vietnamese government and made plans to go to Vietnam - a place that continues to leave scars on the American psyche. They were allowed to go to an orphanage that fall and return with a baby.

The word got out in the Southeast Asian nation, thanks to Annie's parents, that an American couple was coming to adopt a baby. People began bringing babies to Annie's parents for the Americans to adopt; her parents explained that the couple would be adopting from the orphanage.

Then, one day, Jan called Annie's parents in Vietnam to discuss paperwork, and Annie's mother said, "What is your problem? Why did you not call us? We have your baby!"

Jan explained that could not be the case, that they would adopt from the orphanage. Annie's mother replied by telling them the story of the little girl who was in a plastic bowl by the river; a fisherman had found her and taken her to the Truongs, saying "Maybe your daughter and the Americans want this baby."

She was described as being the most beautiful baby the Truongs had ever seen.

Arrangements were quickly made for the Truongs to take care of the baby until the Davidsons could arrive in Doc Von. The Vietnamese government helped out, assuring them the paperwork would be finished within two weeks of her arrival.

Once Annie and Jan (Mark stayed behind in the States) arrived in Ho Chi Minh City (the former Saigon), they faced an 11-hour ride deep into the Doc Von jungles.

When Jan saw her new daughter for the first time, the feeling of joy was almost indescribable.

"It was like nothing I had imagined," she said. "You can't believe someone would leave something so beautiful and valuable to die. My husband and I look at her all the time and say, 'We are so lucky. Out of all the babies left by the side of the river, you became ours.'"

Jan spent three weeks in Vietnam waiting for the paperwork to be finished, but had to return to the U.S. to help take care of her family once she learned there had been a delay. Finally, Jan went back to Vietnam in mid-September to pick up Anna Marie, then made a long trek back to South Carolina via Bangkok, Los Angeles and Atlanta with the new child.

Adopting the baby was not an easy process, but it was a process the Davidsons would be willing to go through again.

Today, the Davidsons have a happy home with their two daughters. The couple is always willing to talk about the process they endured during their quest and to encourage anyone encountering difficulties.

Their advice is not to give up.

"You would have done it, too. I thought about it all day. I'm just glad somebody was there to help him."

- Jim Hunt to a reporter

DAY 12
Life Savers

Wendell Johnson Jr. of Keowee Key, S.C., began one September day much like every other day, except that he was going out to Lake Keowee to help clean up the lake as part of the annual Lake Keowee Sweep.

He was doing his part early because he was going to be out of town during that weekend's volunteer activity. It was late in the afternoon, and Johnson had just finished his last cleanup area and was heading back in his boat when the winds began to blow.

All of a sudden, Johnson looked out and saw trouble develop.

"I saw what looked like two big bubbles out on the lake," he said. "As I got closer, I realized there were three people hanging on to a catamaran, which is a two-hull sailboat.

"The boat had capsized. The mast was 25-30 feet and was all filled with water."

The three people had very little time left before Johnson arrived. The woman in the boat was extremely cold and shivering. Johnson quickly got the lady onto his boat and threw a blanket over her. Then he went on to rescue the other two people.

"Eventually, we pulled the boat and got it level with the water. When the water ran out, we eventually got the sail upright. It took us four tries."

Incredibly, just minutes after struggling for their lives, the men sailed their boat back to shore, where they were camping.

Johnson did not know the names of the trio, but didn't think they lived in the Lake Keowee area.

Johnson wasn't the type who would want to be called a hero; in fact, it's likely I would never have heard about the incident if he hadn't had to fill out a report for Bill Tygihe, one of the coordinators for the Lake Keowee Sweep.

"I think it is outstanding what Wendell did," Tygihe said. "He saved the people's lives on the lake."

Johnson would understand the feelings of Jim Hunt of Westminster, S.C., who one day helped save a man from choking to death.

Hunt probably doesn't consider himself a hero, but in my mind, he became one in a very big way while dining at an area restaurant.

Jim, a commercial pilot for USAir, and his wife, Teena, were having lunch when all of a sudden, Walt Urban of West Union, S.C., began to choke when pieces of food got lodged in his esophagus.

Urban tried to drink something to help get the food down, but the food acted like a dam and cut off his air supply. He motioned for his wife, Laura, to help, but she could not get the food unstuck.

By this time, Hunt had noticed what was going on and rushed to help.

"I saw his wife get up and try to help him and couldn't," Hunt said. "I went over to help and performed the Heimlich maneuver on him. I'd seen it done before, but I had never done it myself."

Quickly, Urban began to breathe again after the close call and retreated to the restroom. He took another drink, and again, the water dammed up inside his throat and he couldn't breathe. This time, Laura was able to help him.

Eventually, an ambulance came and took Urban to the hospital, but by the time he arrived, the food had been dislodged and he was all right.

I called Hunt to talk about what he had done, but he seemed not to want any recognition for his actions.

"You would have done it, too," he said to me. "I did have a good feeling after I did it. It was kind of a feeling of euphoria.

"I thought about it all day. I'm just glad somebody was there to help Walt."

If Hunt hadn't been at the right place at the right time, Walt Urban could have died. In fact, a former newspaper colleague of mine died when he was alone at home and choked on some peanuts.

For those known as first responders, EMTs or paramedics, being at the right place at the right time is routine - regardless of the time of day or night.

Take the case of Brady Grim. He is a firefighter in the Clemson University Fire Department and a South Carolina first responder, which is a person who is first on the scene whenever a medical emergency or an auto accident is reported.

Grim had already worked all night and was home asleep when a call for a first responder was sent out.

A man who had been walking on the indoor track that encircles Clemson's Littlejohn Coliseum had suffered a heart attack and was in jeopardy.

Four people had been on call, and two of them had already responded to another emergency.

Fortunately, Grim lived not very far from Littlejohn, so he immediately jumped out of bed and sprinted as fast as he could to the arena, where he found the man, in his 70s, unconscious.

"He was walking around the track, as he did every day, until he began to have chest pains and started lagging behind the group he was with," Grim said. "He then fell back from the group and collapsed, but his friends thought he had just fainted, and they were unable to really tell me about how serious the situation was."

Grim immediately went to work, starting cardiopulmonary resuscitation (CPR) procedures until more help arrived on the scene. The man was placed on a heart monitor; then it was determined that his heart was fibrillating and his life was in danger.

A defibrillator was immediately placed on the man's heart to shock it back into rhythm. Grim also used two types of medication to speed up the heart's rate and then relax it so it could beat on its own.

As the patient was being loaded onto the ambulance to be taken to the hospital, Grim noticed the man's condition was improving rapidly; he had saved the man from certain death.

Saving a man's life is all part of a day's work for rescue workers, but even Grim admitted he had tears in his eyes while the man was being transported to the hospital.

"Being able to help someone this way makes the inconvenience of the job seem unimportant," he said. "I feel good about what I do."

Three different scenes, three different people, one common outcome: Lives saved because these three, without hesitation, reached out in another person's dire time of need.

"Let us recognize the life of a great soldier, Vivian Tillman,
who passed away this afternoon."

- Dr. Thomas Walker, a pastor in Rocky Mount, N.C., on
the death of community activist Vivian Tillman.

DAY 13

A Soldier for the Community

In every community, there are always those who want to do whatever it takes to make life better for everyone, regardless of race, creed or color.

Vivian Tillman of Rocky Mount, N.C., was one such person. Tillman died in 1993 at the age of 75. Vivian's column, "Community Upbeat," had not appeared in the paper for some time, and, ironically, earlier in the week, there had been a call about its absence.

In conversation with Tillman's daughter, Kim, I learned that Vivian was very ill, so we printed a response relaying the news, also saying we expected the column to resume very quickly.

It was the first time many people in the community knew that Vivian was ill.

"She was a very private person," Kim told me.

Vivian had been obviously sick for a long time, but had never really showed her pain when visiting the newspaper office.

During the previous 2 1/2 years, I had gotten to know Vivian very well. Her Sunday column was extremely popular in the community.

"In her weekly article, she managed to pick up the little tidbits happening in the community," said Tarboro (N.C.) City Schools board member Dr. Clifford Coleman. "She had a tremendous readership to her column. I have, on occasion, visited her home, and the latest articles and clippings were all around the place."

Vivian would normally come to the paper during our early-morning deadline period about 8:30 or 9 a.m. She would always deliver the column to me personally and say a few words.

Those who know about newspaper deadlines realize that at 8:30 or 9, we would be racing around to make sure we published on time, trying to capture the latest news. It was a struggle to be patient with people when they came in at that time of day.

But with Vivian, our brief time every week was always entertaining and usually informative. Her smile sure helped break the pressure of morning deadlines.

Several staffers came to me after finding out she died. "Vivian was really 75?" one staffer asked. Her smile, figure and attire kept her looking much younger than her 75 years.

Perhaps what I appreciated most was her commitment to the black community, the Democratic Party, the various organizations with which she was affiliated and her column.

Vivian and I communicated a lot during 2 1/2 years. When I first arrived in Rocky Mount, I asked the names of community leaders who would be good news sources. Vivian's name was mentioned as one such contact.

We called on Vivian several times to write front-page columns, sometimes on touchy race issues. She always came through.

We contacted Vivian numerous times for the proper sources with different stories. Vivian would make a few phone calls and usually come to the paper with typed names and phone numbers of potential contacts.

During a voter-registration rally with Rev. Jesse Jackson at a packed local church, the pastor of the church, Dr. Thomas L. Walker, called on the congregation of 1,200 people for a moment of silence.

"Let us recognize the life of a great soldier, Vivian Tillman, who passed away this afternoon," Walker said. When he spoke those words, a collective "ah" went through the crowd, and the silence was held until the political speeches continued.

Kim Tillman said the best word to describe her mother was "an organizer."

"She was always an educator, not necessarily in terms of the school system, but if she had information she had come across or something she had read, she shared it. She was a very committed person."

"It was my pleasure to know her for many years," said Fred Turnage, then the Rocky Mount mayor. "She was deeply and generously interested in the city and the area. She was greatly dedicated and put in a lot of energy in city affairs as a teacher, community volunteer and in work with her sorority (Sigma Gamma Rho).

"She did a tremendous amount of work to improve the community."

Coles described Vivian as "a very special kind of person. She was dedicated, motivated and service-oriented. Early in her career, she was a teacher.

"The years I've known her, she was very active in politics. She made the Democratic Party more visible and more accessible. Voter registration grew rapidly, thanks to her efforts. As a person, she was very friendly and accessible. She will certainly be missed. She was always beautifully dressed and always a delight to see. She had a pleasant smile, no matter what."

Vivian's final column was published in August 1992. I looked back on a few of her columns before writing about her.

At the conclusion of her Aug. 2, 1992, effort, she talked about native son Arthur Barnes preparing to play at The Wright's Center in Rocky Mount that day.

She said, "The summer's hotter than ever, and it gets even hotter with the sounds of jazz...Help us keep jazz alive in Rocky Mount, plan to come today! The set begins at Brown's on Highland Avenue in Rocky Mount."

This was typical Vivian. Always promoting Rocky Mount. Always smiling and always upbeat.

Her column's title, Community Upbeat, was appropriate.

There is no other way to say what Vivian's loss meant to the community than to repeat what Turnage told me.

"Dan, she is sorely missed," he said.

"You can share a story or let them know you care."
- Jim Burns on how he helps patients at the hospital where
he volunteers.

DAY 14
Giving Back to Home

─────────────

The scene is in the Oconee Memorial Hospital emergency room in Seneca, S.C. The room is already bustling when another patient is wheeled in.

The patient has had a diabetic seizure and is sprouting tubes from his arms. The patient gazes up from his ordeal and sees a familiar face.

The face is that of Jim Burns, an OMH Auxiliary volunteer. Burns spends the next few minutes comforting the patient, who is reassured by the concern for his situation and Jim's sincerity.

******

Jim Burns is one of those people who makes a difference in communities across the nation, both large and small.

I should know, because in the above scene, I was the patient. My blood sugar had plunged too low and I had been taken to the hospital.

Burns can be found each week with his wife, Reva, volunteering his services to the OMH Auxiliary. He performs countless volunteer acts day in and day out, regardless of the season.

Both Jim and Reva are scheduled one day each week at the hospital, but Jim usually volunteers more of his time each week. His current project is working with both patients and parking at the facility, which in January

1996, was undergoing an expansion project. Burns used a golf cart donated to the Auxiliary to transport both patients and visitors from the hospital's temporary parking lot to the facility.

Burns retired from Clemson University in 1984 as the director of the Communications Center at the school. He had always volunteered his time for many worthy projects both on- and off-campus, but went at it full-force following his retirement from CU.

"I had a lot more time to do this type of thing after I retired," Burns said. "I really enjoy the Auxiliary. I enjoy the brief personal relationship with the patients who come to the hospital.

"You can share a little story or let them know you care. I think it helps the patients and families. I make every attempt I can to be personable with everyone who comes in."

Jan Crismore, who heads the OMH Auxiliary, says Jim is a dedicated, reliable volunteer.

"He is one person I can always ask to do something, and I know it will get done," Crismore said.

Burns recalled two experiences while working on the front desk that have stayed with him since he began volunteering his time in 1989. One of those incidents involved a pregnant woman who came to the emergency room one day.

"The man and woman were foreign students from Clemson and pulled into the parking lot," said Burns. "He told me, 'My wife is having a baby.' I told him to bring the car around to the front, while I called the OB/GYN ward and a wheelchair. The woman wound up having a 6-pound baby just five minutes later," Burns recalled. "It was a very close call."

Another time, Burns recalled an incident when a visitor from Florida came into the hospital with his wife. The man followed the signs to OMH after his wife experienced chest pains.

"Again, I was sitting at the front desk," said Burns. "I brought the woman in with a wheelchair while he parked the car. He parked the car and within four or five minutes we got her into the emergency room and the doctor was already working on her. He told me, 'This is hard to believe. A stranger comes to town by hospital signs and after arriving at the hospital the patient is being examined by a physician five minutes later.' He was so thankful."

Jim has always remembered Matthew 25:37-39, a Biblical passage which reads: "Then the righteous will answer him, 'Lord, when did we see you hungry and feed you, or thirsty and give you something to drink? When did we see you a stranger and invite you in, or needing clothes and clothe you? When did we see you sick or in prison and go to visit you?'"

"I believe in that passage," Burns said. "I'm not a pious Paul, but I think about those verses often."

Burns has not been without his own adversity in life. In 1980, Burns nearly died after undergoing open-heart surgery.

"I had a regular physical exam and had a stress test," said Burns. "During the stress test, it showed a dramatic difference from the year before. I received a catheterization the next day."

"That experience made me aware of the more important things in life," he said. "I am so thankful today for the opportunity to work with other people. There have been many times in my own life where other people have come forward and helped me.

"I guess this is one of my ways of giving back."

Burns had another heart catheterization in February 1996. The doctors again discovered the problem in a stress test. This time around, he had a triple-bypass operation and was lucky to survive.

"I am very blessed," Burns said. "I realize how fragile life is. I am back to being active again and feeling as good as I ever have."

And again, Burns is back volunteering his time at the hospital and in his Millbrook neighborhood.

One of his Millbrook neighbors told me even after the 1996 heart surgery, Jim immediately went back working on the area.

Crismore said Jim always goes out of his way to look for things to make it more pleasurable for a patient's visit.

"He always has an eye for people who need help and is there to give it," Crismore said. "Jim will be our hospital auxiliary president next year. I know he will do it very capably."

Crismore said Jim has great compassion for others.

"Jim has had some ups and downs in his own life," Crismore said. "I think those ups and downs have made him more aware of other people's needs."

Giving back is something Jim has always done, probably more than almost anyone else around him. Burns is a firm believer that everyone should donate time to whatever cause they feel strongest about.

TODAY'S QUOTE:

"Our challenge is to bring sunshine into a very dreary day."
**- Skip Sprye on why he volunteers with
the Make-A-Wish Foundation**

DAY 15

Guardian Angels

A guardian angel is traditionally said to be a person assigned by God to protect a person from harm.

Guardian angels are always said to be over a person's shoulder, ready to act on a moment's notice.

It is unlikely many people have come face-to-face with a guardian angel, although some people in eastern North Carolina might dispute that contention, especially those who have dealt with Skip and Faye Sprye.

Skip and Faye have been extremely active in the Make-A-Wish Foundation of Eastern North Carolina since the late 1980s. Their impact on the lives of suffering children and families has been more than profound.

"Our challenge is to bring sunshine into a very dreary day," said Skip. "We take a child's wish referred to us by a parent or doctor and make it come true.

"Some have simple wishes. Others are more difficult. The hardest ones are those dealing with celebrities."

Wishes can be granted and happen virtually overnight or can take days or weeks.

Once, I went to Skip and Faye on one of their visits. We met at a restaurant a few blocks from the government housing projects in Rocky Mount. As we entered the projects, I was overwhelmed with the sights before my eyes. The houses were very dilapidated and did not look to be fit to live in.

When we walked to the front door of the wish recipient, the screen in the door was caved in and the house was quite warm. Inside was a bubbly teen-ager about to receive her wish to go shopping.

A few days later, for the first time, the girl was able to go on a shopping spree and purchase anything she wanted at the stores inside the local mall, thanks to the Make-A-Wish Foundation.

It was unbelievable seeing how the girl's face lit up when she walked through the mall and could buy anything she wanted.

I was amazed at how compassionate both Skip and Faye were throughout the whole process. They are both highly successful people, but they are not afraid to go to the downtrodden areas of their community and work to help others.

Skip first heard of Make-A-Wish at a 1986 Million Dollar Round Table meeting. "The president of Make-A-Wish, Tommy Austin, was on the platform that year," Skip said. "He really inspired me. He was a federal treasury agent who traveled across the country to promote Make-A-Wish. At the time, we didn't have any Make-A-Wish chapters in North Carolina."

Skip, who owns Sprye & Associates, a financial services business specializing in life insurance, was active in the Rocky Mount community at the time. Because of many commitments, he had to put the thought of working in the Make-A-Wish organization on hold.

Skip and Faye finally became active in wish-granting in 1988.

In the beginning, Skip approached the Hardee's corporation and attempted to show Make-A-Wish's broad-reaching impact.

"Hardee's gave $350,000 nationally over a three-year period to Make-A-Wish," Skip said of his contact with the North Carolina-based hamburger giant. "I went on several trips with John Merritt (then a Hardee's executive) attempting to convince him this should be one of Hardee's national emphasis points as far as being a corporate citizen."

The Raleigh chapter has since granted numerous wishes, averaging $3,500 each; children who are granted wishes must have a life-threatening illness.

"Even if a nurse calls, we need a referral from the family and a doctor," Skip said. "Generally, the children are from 2 1/2 to 18 years old.

"When we are contacted about a wish, we contact the doctor directly to make sure the illness is life-threatening. If the doctor says yes, then the Raleigh wish coordinator picks somebody to handle the wish.

"They assign people like us to go out and visit with the child. Generally, the two of us go out and talk to the child and parents. We establish what the wish is.

"No wish is denied because of financial cost. Then we put the wish together, depending on the necessity of expediency."

Skip and Faye enjoy the time they spend together in Make-A-Wish. "I love being involved in this great organization for so many reasons," Faye said, "partly because Skip and I do this as a team. One of us will interview the parents and the other will talk with the child separately.

"This is done to make sure the child expresses his or her own wish without pressure or input from the parents."

Faye says she is often asked how it is possible to get involved with a youth who has a life-threatening illness.

"By the time we meet these children, they have gone through more than most adults go through in a lifetime," Faye said. "We are a bright spot in their lives because they know what the Make-A-Wish Foundation represents, and that is to grant wishes.

"The anticipation of going to Disney World, meeting a celebrity, receiving a Nintendo, computer or whatever their wish might be brings a happiness in their lives that, for a moment, makes them forget about the needles, chemotherapy and doctor visits."

Faye told me there is not anything more beautiful and heart-warming than to see the smiles on the faces of the kids who have, for so long, experienced a lot of pain - emotionally and physically.

"For parents, there is sometimes a burden financially to be able to afford anything extra for their child as a result of the illness. To know a wish is being granted to their daughter or son is overwhelming," Faye said. "They open their hearts to you, just like anyone would when someone is doing something special for your child.

"This is why Skip and I love being volunteers for Make-A-Wish."

Skip did a presentation one time at a Rocky Mount Kiwanis Club meeting in which he showed a video of what Make-A-Wish was all about. When he introduced the video, he said he doubted there would be a dry eye in the house when the video ended.

I think he was right.

Skip and Faye have continued to be active in Make-A-Wish since my departure from Rocky Mount. In fact, Faye reports they are as busy as ever during the first part of 1996.

"We just had a boy, Thomas, go to Disney World," she said.

Faye recalled a touching experience with one of their clients who had gone blind because of cancer.

"The child was a wonderful, wonderful person," she said. "I was visiting his house and he took me into each room, to each window, and told me to feel the warmth of the sunshine on my face. There are so many things we all take for granted."

Another recent wish took a Fayetteville, N.C., youngster with a brain tumor to see the Mighty Morphin Power Rangers on the set in California.

Faye says she and Skip plan to continue their Make-A-Wish work for years and years to come.

"Dealing with the families is never depressing for us," she said. "We are the bright spots in their lives."

The Make-A-Wish organization is truly one of the best charities going. Skip and Faye Sprye deserve so much credit for what they have done for others in their times of suffering.

I believe they may be their area's answer to guardian angels for sick and suffering children.

Here I am with my personal angel, my best friend — and now, my wife. I met Victoria Stokley at a concert in June 1995, and we have yet to let go of each other. We almost didn't meet that night, but I believe a higher power must have guided us toward each other.

Tony Sample didn't let a disabled arm bother him — he became a top-notch athlete, hitting better than .400 on the baseball team his senior year in high school. He later became a good bowler, with two 300 games to his credit and even taking part in a PBA tournament.

Vivian Tillman was active in many causes in Rocky Mount, N.C. Her involvement in the community endeared her to many people and made her an icon — as well as an angel.

Dorothy Cox has been involved in a personal battle with Alzheimer's disease for some time now. She is shown with her friend Mildred Davis, who suffered a stroke.

Donna Gustavel suffers from cerebral palsy and has undergone many hardships in her life. Doctors didn't expect her to live much past 20, but now, in her early 40s, she is a courageous example of how someone can beat the odds.

Brian Compton had all sorts of birth defects when he was born. But these problems have not stopped his kind and generous spirit. His courage even earned him a Hero of the Day award from a South Carolina television station.

Ashley McCoy lost a wallet with $289 in it while on a New York school trip. She thought the money was gone forever ... until fashion executive Jake Einhorn found it and sent her a check covering the amount she lost.

Norman Lambert has been a football coach, a family man ... and the owner of Lambert's Cafe, perhaps the happiest restaurant in all of Southeast Missouri. Yet his generous spirit has meant more to people than all of the "throwed rolls" his eatery serves.

Mike Rodgers was a salesman for a South Carolina chemical company when a truck accident nearly took his life. Today, as a Salvation Army minister, he and his wife, Susan, reach out to the poor and needy in Oconee County.

Evelyn Coggins had always wanted to play the violin as a child, but circumstances prevented it. After her husband's death, Coggins, now in her 80s, began taking lessons and has become a skilled player. She is shown with her instructor, Peter Moore.

Nick (left) and Mayo Boddie are two Rocky Mount, N.C., businessmen who bought one of the first franchised Hardee's restaurants and became the company's second largest franchisee. Yet they have not forgotten their eastern North Carolina roots.

Adam and Marguerite Rumoshosky have been together for more than 50 years. In that time, Adam has accomplished much — including establishing a successful anti-littering organization in Oconee County, S.C., based on the Keep America Beautiful program.

Billy Mills won a gold medal for the United States in the 1964 Tokyo Olympic Games. His own story, coming from a difficult upbringing in South Dakota to a successful life, has been an inspiration both to me and countless others over the past 30-plus years.

Patricia encountered many problems during her troubled childhood before being taken in by Anne and Joe Rackley and the Collins Children's Home at the tender age of 5 years.

A decade later, Patrica has grown from a shy, unsure child into a beautiful young woman. The love and guidance given to her by the home literally turned her life around.

Amber Langston (center) and her parents, Wendy (left) and Bruce (second right), have gone through what most people would consider a nightmare — leukemia. However, Amber's spirited nature has helped her defeat what would have, at one time, been a deadly enemy.

Warren and Ellie Detrick didn't let naysayers get in the way of their dreams. Warren invented a device he called Multi-Board — a reusable white board, with erasable color markers, that has become standard office equipment in many offices around the world.

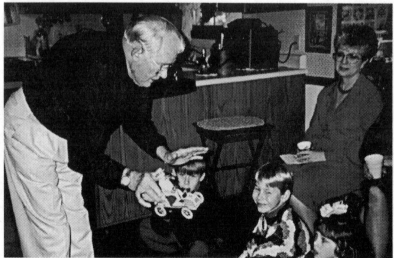

Warren has become one of the most ardent supporters of the Collins Children's Home, showing off his collection of antique toys and performing magic tricks for the children each holiday season. The visit is always a much-anticipated event each December.

Anne and Joe Rackley (right), along with their daughter, Kimberly, turned their Seneca, S.C., home into a haven for abused and neglected children — the Collins Children's Home. Kimberly and her husband, Mike Kunz, continue to help her parents as they provide hope and a home for many children.

75

Countess Jeanne-Marie Dickens was an orphan and refugee during World War II. Now married into the Charles Dickens family, she helps to promote the memory of what the famous author stood for and helps charities throughout the world.

Warren Detrick's Multi-Board has many uses — including a wish of happiness from Warren and Ellie to Victoria and me during a recent visit. Warren is one of the most selfless, giving people I have ever met.

"The Lord was really looking out for me. I felt a strong call to go into the ministry when I was a kid. I kept getting the call, and while recovering from the accident, it gave me time to think. I felt that going into the Salvation Army ministry is what He wanted me to do."

- Mike Rodgers on the auto accident that nearly claimed his life

DAY 16
Battling Back

Looking at Mike Rodgers, one would assume he is just another person trying to further the work of The Salvation Army.

In many ways, one might be right.

Underneath the friendly, calm surface, though, are indications of another battle Rodgers once fought and won.

A battle to stay alive.

You see, Salvation Army Lt. Mike Rodgers can count himself lucky to be alive at all.

Several years ago, he was pulled from the wreckage of a truck he was driving for a chemical company in Sumter, S.C.

"I had just been promoted as a manager of distribution, warehousing and manufacturing at the company," Rodgers recalled, "and the company wanted me to drive a truck to get some first-hand experience on how the trucks worked if I ever had to hire a new driver.

"It was just a one-shot deal for me and the company; I'll tell you, that was some shot!"

The plan had called for Rodgers to drive a truck to the first delivery stop one of the regular drivers was to make that day, with the regular driver taking over after that. Rodgers was making a left turn into another company's delivery area when an 18-wheeler suddenly came bearing down on Rodgers.

The truck, which was estimated to be traveling at 75 mph, smashed into the side of Rodgers' truck, completely fracturing the left side of his body and knocking him into, as he said, la-la land.

"I really don't remember much about the wreck, and maybe that's good," Rodgers said.

"I've been told the entire side where I was sitting was crushed, and the entire left side of my body was broken up like a smashed cookie."

Rodgers was taken to Charleston, S.C., and underwent seven-and-a-half hours of surgery to insert steel plates in his arm and rods in his legs to aid in recovery. He was in traction for two-and-a-half months and underwent therapy for a year in order to relearn how to walk.

"They had to do a hip replacement operation, they had to put plates and rods in my leg; I was a mess," Rodgers said.

Most people would likely have been killed in such a devastating crash; Rodgers, however, believes that someone upstairs was looking out for him that day.

"The Lord was really looking out for me," Rodgers said. "I had felt a strong call to go into the ministry when I was a kid. I had been going to a Baptist church school since I was 11, then started attending Salvation Army services when I was 15.

"I kept getting the call, and while I was recovering from the accident, it gave me a lot of time to think. I felt that going into the Salvation Army ministry was what He wanted me to do."

Rodgers and his wife, Susan, arrived in Seneca, S.C. in mid-1995 and have been very active in the ministry and community since coming. The couple had been married about three years at the time of his accident.

"Susan has always been very supportive," said Mike. "I had to learn to walk with a walker, then crutches after the accident. She was always there encouraging me, even on my down days.

"Everything has been a challenge. For a long time, I had been working within the Lord's permissive will, but not his perfect will," Rodgers recalled. "Now that has all changed."

The challenge in Seneca may have been as difficult as recovering from the near-fatal crash. When Mike and Susan arrived in Seneca, The Salvation Army's reputation had dwindled to a point where financial support was only sparse.

Mike and Susan immediately stepped in and started working to restore that tarnished image.

"The thrift store was not as organized as it should have been and wasn't up to Salvation Army standards," Mike said. "Now, we have a computer system which keeps all our books and we can chart our income vs. expense. The actual look of the thrift store was initially poor and trashy. We have tried to change that."

When the time came for the annual bell-ringing campaign, Mike wanted to see the fund-raiser done with volunteers. During the previous year, The Salvation Army had to *pay* people to ring bells, which is against the Army's philosophy.

"We even heard that one person was smoking cigarettes at one of the kettles the year before," Mike said. "That is totally against what The Salvation Army is all about."

Mike's efforts to obtain volunteers worked, thereby raising $11,000 extra at Christmas time for the unfortunate in Oconee County. Thanks to those efforts, it was a pleasant Christmas time for many families in need.

Mike says he has learned a lot during this ordeal that nearly cost him his life.

"My life at that moment could have ended," he said. "I realize in life you are not promised anything. Our lives are controlled and led by the Lord.

"I think we have had an impact in Oconee County. There are so many other things The Salvation Army can do that we hope to eventually accomplish here."

When it came time to salute volunteers at an annual recognition banquet, Mike and Susan stole the show. Those in attendance gave them a standing ovation for their efforts to help Oconee County.

"It was quite a night," Mike said. "I guess it showed us how much the community does appreciate what we have done over the last year."

"A little bit of lust, a little bit of sin feeds like a gator at your fingertips and tries to consume you. You have to put it off and completely get away from it. If you are committed to Jesus, you can put them off."

- Hall Thorpe, who ministers to prisoners

DAY 17
Ministering to Prisoners

Life in prison is hard for the average person to imagine.

Picture being in a cell the majority of the time, bed-to-bed with other inmates. Imagine having a shower and restroom facilities with no curtain.

Consider this as a daily ritual: Having to rise at 5:30 a.m. with a head count, followed by breakfast. The remainder of the day consists of working from 7:30 a.m.-4 p.m., with lunch included, then returning to a cellblock after dinner.

The day's pay ranges from 40 cents to a dollar, depending on the job. The money goes toward purchasing toothpaste, cigarettes and other small items.

Prison life was hard for me to visualize until a trip one wintry day with a Rocky Mount, N.C., gospel ministry to Caledonia Correctional Institute in North Carolina.

"You'll have to go through several barred doors before you make it all the way in," said Rocky Mount resident George Moore, one of those who participates in the weekly ministry sessions at the prison. "I hope you aren't claustrophobic."

Moore was correct about the several doors with bars. The prison trip did reveal that Caledonia had a top-notch group of guards who seemed to sincerely care about their work. The guards were helpful, professional and friendly. Inside the prison, it was warm, but well-kept.

Our long trek finally led to a room of worship for the prisoners.

About 20 prisoners were seated when we arrived, prepared for the worship service with Moore, Hall Thorpe, John Minges and prison chaplain Austin Anderson of Lake Gaston, N.C.

Upon arrival, the prisoners all gave a big hug to the ministers and me. Moore forewarned me, saying, "I hope this type of hugging doesn't bother you."

It was evident immediately that those attending the service were sincere, from the first handshake and hug.

Moore read from the book of Numbers, telling the story of how naysayers talked Israelites into not going into the promised land for 40 years. "They were miserable and they died before they got into the promised land," Moore told the prisoners. "The story behind it is we can't let others tell us what to do but listen to the Lord.

"Millions of Israelites wandered in the wilderness for 40 years because they didn't have faith."

Thorpe followed Moore and spoke of Colossians, chapter 3.

"This chapter starts off with a big word, If," said Thorpe, in a loud, inspiring tone. "It's up to us...

"A little bit of lust, a little bit of sin feeds like a gator at your fingertips and tries to consume you. You have to put it off and completely get away from it. If you are committed to Jesus, you *can* put them off."

Next, Minges spoke of a trip across Maine. The inmates were captivated by Minges' vivid descriptions of the trip, and probably for a few moments, felt as if they were riding along in person.

After the service, Vernon Blackhorse and Wesley Shuler, a pair of inmates, stopped and chatted. The two were personable and articulate. Their responses to questions came with ease and sincerity. Both seemed to have turned their lives around during their prison stays.

"I come every Wednesday and Thursday to service," Blackhorse said. "I would rather be up here than in the yard. Here, it is an opportunity to sit and listen. This definitely shows me how I should have lived."

"Most of all, you get the word of God when you come here," Shuler added. "Coming here helps me throughout the week and makes me feel good every day."

After the talk with the inmates, we headed into an office room to converse with Chaplain Anderson. On the way, we toured a block which housed several inmates. A television was on, and a few prisoners were playing cards on a tattered, but sturdy, card table.

The inmates were docile, with little horseplay. Moore and the others carried on conversations with several inmates.

The trek down the block made me realize one thing - I never want to serve time. If only we could take those who have the potential to sell drugs, or kill, and let them take a similar tour, it is doubtful they would want to spend the rest of their lives in such a cramped environment with little, if any, freedom or privacy.

When we sat in Anderson's office, he revealed some startling statistics. "Only 20 percent of those who are Christians come back to prison after they are released," Anderson said. "Of those who are not Christians, 75 percent come back."

Anderson seemed to be one of the most genuine chaplains I have ever met. "He just really goes out of his way," said Thorpe. "He is the most dedicated person I have ever seen. He makes us feel welcome."

After about 20 minutes in the office area, we concluded our visit. It was nice to see the barred doors open and to walk into the cold, but fresh, night air.

The thought then crossed my mind. "Why would someone want to do anything that would strip their freedoms and put them behind bars?"

Then, I shot a glance at Moore, Thorpe and Minges. These men don't get paid for what they do. For years, they have driven through rain, sleet and snow to visit the prisoners each week, lifting up their spirits and spreading the Gospel.

And, I'll bet there are several prisoners who have turned their lives around, all because those Rocky Mount men took time out to care.

"The Lord expects you to take care of the ones who need it. We are the Lord's arms and legs."

- Pat Lee on her efforts to start a soup kitchen.

DAY 18

Extending a Helping Hand

One of the most inspirational stories in the Bible is the one where Christ and his disciples feed 5,000 hungry people bread and fish.

In this Biblical reference in Matthew, chapters 14-21, Jesus and his disciples were preaching in Galilee, with thousands of followers in attendance. The multitudes had listened to preaching all day and were extremely hungry. One of the disciples went to Jesus and told him the predicament. Jesus responded by asking, "What do you have?"

The disciple said one boy had five loaves of bread and two fish in his lunch basket. The disciple brought the boy's food to Jesus and told those in attendance to all be seated. Jesus lifted up the lunch and offered a prayer, saying, "Lord, bless this food." The disciples then distributed from that lunch. Jesus and the disciples fed all 5,000 people that day and even collected leftovers.

Pat Lee of Walhalla, S.C., must have been paying attention when that story was discussed or read in her Sunday school class, because she has always had a soft heart for the needy.

Lee, who owns a business in the Keowee Key area, began her volunteer work by sponsoring some less fortunate families during recent holiday seasons. But the most impacting volunteer effort for her occurs on Thanksgiving Day, when a Seneca group known as Feed the 5,000 serves traditional turkey dinners to the poor, homeless and anyone else who needs a dinner. In addition, volunteers give away clothes to the needy during the celebration.

"Once, a man came needing a pair of shoes," Lee said. "His feet were cracked open and bleeding. I also watched some people eat with their hands like they had never eaten before.

"I knew after that Thanksgiving I had to do more."

Lee's response was to organize an effort to start a local soup kitchen, which would be called Our Daily Bread.

"We had a meeting recently; 55-60 people were there," Lee said of her initial efforts. "We elected a board of directors, had a lot of donations, established bylaws and got insurance in place."

Then came the stumbling block - finding a building to house the soup kitchen. For several weeks, Lee was unable to get anyone to commit to a facility. Lee and the other Our Daily Bread organizers wanted the kitchen to be somewhere in the vicinity of downtown Seneca, an idea which did not sit well with some people in the city.

Lee keenly feels the need to help the less fortunate in Oconee County. "One day, I was driving through downtown Seneca looking for a possible place for the soup kitchen, and I saw two people rummaging through a business' garbage can for food. It is not right that people should have to dig in garbage to eat," Lee said.

One might think an area like Oconee and Pickens counties, S.C., would not have the problems with the hungry and homeless that larger cities such as, say, New York, Charlotte, Atlanta or St. Louis might have. Believe it or not, nothing could be further from the truth.

Unfortunately, many people have buried their heads in the sand and refused to admit such a problem exists.

I think often, people believe the needy or homeless chose their way, but that is not always true. Some have mental or physical disabilities which prevent them from working and having a normal life.

To put her idea in motion, Lee approached a well-known area businessman who always has a giving spirit. The businessman agreed to help Lee in her effort, pledging $100 a month to get the ball rolling.

Since then, more and more funds and business support have been incoming to establish Our Daily Bread.

Lee's efforts were not universally accepted; in fact, many opposed the idea, saying it would bring what they believed would be "the wrong element" to downtown.

Lee's response to these nay-sayers was direct and to the point.

"People can close their eyes to this, but I believe we have to come to grips with it and show we are a loving, caring community."

By early April 1996, Lee had been battling for several days trying to find a facility for Our Daily Bread. She had become depressed because no one seemed to want to come forward.

"I kept praying, but I was down about it," said Lee. "I was starting to wonder if it was ever going to happen."

Then one day, Dr. Henry Salter telephoned Lee. He volunteered to lease a portion of his building in Seneca's Main Street.

"Dr. Salter called me and said he didn't have any idea I didn't have a place for the soup kitchen until he read the articles and editorials in the *Journal/Tribune* newspaper," said Lee. "This was an answer to our prayers. Dr. Salter plans to lease us the whole back side of the building, which is 1,500 square feet, for as long as we want."

Lee expects the kitchen to be clean and professional, adding to the ever-progressing atmosphere of downtown Seneca. She said the kitchen will be open from noon-2 p.m. each day.

Lee has had a simple philosophy throughout the entire process of organizing the soup kitchen and battling those who didn't believe in her vision:

"The Lord expects you to take care of the ones who need it. We are the Lord's arms and legs."

DAY 19

A Strong Heart Beats Alzheimer's

They say one can judge a lot about a person by his or her heart.

Dorothy Cox of Oakway, S.C., has a heart about as big as they come.

The 69-year-old Cox showed her love for other people when she raised $1,900 in the fall of 1995 for the annual Alzheimer's Foundation Memory Walk. Cox had the highest individual fund-raising total for the walk in the Upstate region of South Carolina.

Cox visited every business, friend and church acquaintance she could think of to raise funds for the Alzheimer's cause.

First of all, I don't know how someone could say no to Cox's infectious smile or her wonderful personality, but in some cases, she has even baked bread and pound cakes for donors.

Diane Parsons, Cox's daughter and director of nutritional services for Mariner Health Care in Seneca, S.C., said she was very proud of her mother for her efforts.

Parsons told me Cox's sister, Florence Meeks, is dealing with her husband, Charles, who has Alzheimer's in its early stages. Cox often assists her sister in caring for Charles.

"I'd give everything I own to help find a cure for Alzheimer's," Cox said. "People do not realize just how hard this disease is on other people. I watch Charles pack every day, thinking he's going somewhere. He doesn't even realize he's at home.

"He was once a college professor. He constantly talks about things that happened in his younger days."

Cox's motiviation is simple. "I love people," she said. "I feel like I can't do enough to help others. It's been very hard on me since my husband died (March 31, 1988). He was a real sweetheart. I love to make people feel good."

Mariner Health Care Administrator Pam Smith said Cox gives her full attention to the people she visits.

"I can't tell you how many loaves of bread and pound cakes she has baked for people," Parsons added.

Parsons was glad to see her mother become interested in a project. "I am so happy about how the fund-raiser went," she told me. "I know how important it is to find a cure for those who are suffering from the disease."

Cox said that one donor she contacted drove an hour from Cashiers, N.C., to participate in the walk.

Cox had three $100 donors - Seneca Mayor Johnny Fields, church acquaintance Betty Spearman and Cox's sister, Florence. Mayor Fields was so impressed by Cox that he couldn't help but donate a large amount of money. Spearman donated in memory of her mother, who has the disease.

Another special donor was Bill Smith, who operates Jim Smith Garage in Westminster. Cox's husband used to have their car fixed by Jim Smith, Bill's father; Jim suffered with Alzheimer's until his death.

Cox said Bill gave her a $50 bill for the cause without batting an eye. He told her he wanted to do it in memory of his father. Cox went back after the walk and gave Bill Smith an Alzheimer's Walk T-shirt and a thank-you card.

Cox plans to walk again in 1996 for Alzheimer's; I'd be willing to bet that once again, she will top the fund-raising list. She has seen firsthand the perils of Alzheimer's by taking care of Charles Meeks.

Three times a week, Cox visits Mariner Health Care in Seneca. "I see Miss Cox pushing patients around and spending a lot of one-on-one time with patients," she said. "She does a lot of things the staff does not have time to do. It does a lot to lift their spirits. She is a very caring person."

One of the people Cox constantly works with is stroke patient Mildred Davis. Mildred cannot speak, but understands all that is said to her.

I met both ladies one day at my newspaper office parking lot. Cox had Davis in the car with her, and they were on their way to a shopping mall.

Cox told me she does not like to see Davis and others like her remain in the home with no outside stimuli. When I went out to the car to meet Davis, Cox asked Davis if she would join her in singing a song to me. I almost cried when the two ladies grabbed me by the hand and began to attempt to sing the most touching rendition of *Jingle Bells* I have ever heard.

Sara Brown is another Mariner resident who Cox visits. Brown was one of Cox's elementary-school teachers.

One of the kindest cards I have ever received came after I had written a column praising Cox for what she had done for other people.

"You made it a rainbow day! You know how hard it is for me to take praise; sometimes, I don't feel like I deserve it. Please continue to pray for me, that I can make happy days for these lovely people. I feel I am the lucky one, getting to be with these guys. I love all these guys. Thank you and God bless, Dorothy Cox.

"P.S. You know, because of the stroke, Mildred can't read. I cut the column out of the paper and read it to her. Now it is on the wall in her room. Mildred cried. If you noticed, she also signed this card, in red. I think this means 'I Love You.'"

Last Thanksgiving, when it was time to walk for diabetes, guess who was at the head of the line?

Dorothy Cox, of course.

I admire Cox because she is committed not only to Alzheimer's, but to any charitable cause. I especially admire her for taking time each day for thinking of others in the elderly population who are less fortunate than she.

"For a long time, we didn't have much money...he (Norman) would always pick up the check whenever I would bring my family in. If it hadn't been for that, I don't know if I could have taken my family out to eat."

- A Sikeston, Mo., resident on Norman Lambert, founder of Lambert's Cafe

DAY 20
Home of the 'Throwed Rolls'

In my book, tradition means a lot.

Like many communities, Sikeston, Mo., has many traditions, from rodeos to carnivals to pageants.

But the best-known tradition in Sikeston, besides the annual rodeo, is Lambert's Cafe.

During my 1988-90 stay in Sikeston, anytime I ventured outside the Missouri Bootheel region I was always asked about "that eatin' joint that serves the hot rolls."

What was so unusual about those rolls wasn't that they were made differently from other rolls, but that they were thrown from various points in the restaurant to a patron's table. The rolls quickly became known as "throwed rolls."

Whenever friends or relatives visited Sikeston, I always had to make a trip to Lambert's, even if everyone in my party had to stand in line for an hour.

One time, rumors were flying around that Lambert's had been sold. I tracked down Norman Lambert, the owner of the cafe, and found the rumors to be untrue.

He admitted that he had been approached by representatives of the late country music singer Conway Twitty about franchising the restaurant, but nothing else came of the discussion; he also admitted that a number of lucrative offers came his way, either to expand or to sell his name to a franchise operation.

Norman Lambert is one of the nicest, most genuine people I have met in my 35 years. Even with his success, he is as "down to earth" as anyone I have ever known.

"I love people," the 62-year-old Lambert told me. "What matters is your friends and people. My mother and father struggled in the beginning. I also know what it is like to struggle. I guess that has given me a great deal of compassion for the poor."

A lot of people don't know this, but Norman donates complimentary meals to or always picks up the tab for anyone who is disabled or physically challenged. He makes it very easy for people with disabilities to visit his place of business.

Norman has a philosophy about business much different than "corporate America." Norman doesn't budget in 2 percent for media advertising, but gives the money back to customers by picking up the tab for some people.

"If somebody scratches your back and does something nice for you, you ought to do something back for them," Lambert said. "This helps me say thank you to the customers. It is the least I can do. Every major chain takes 2 percent of their revenues and puts it into advertising. I take that 2 percent and give it back to the customer. I believe 99.9 percent of people are good."

After I had written some articles about Lambert's, he refused to let me pay whenever I came in. It reached the point where I was almost embarrassed to go in because each time he took care of my check, regardless if I had two or eight people in my crowd. I remember taking my family there once and just having a few dollars in my pocket, barely enough to cover the check. Norman came and got my ticket. I guess he never knew how much that gesture meant to me.

A neighbor told me a similar story.

"For a long time, we didn't have much money," he told me. "Norman was a friend of the family, and he would always pick up the check whenever I would bring my family in. He'll never know how much that meant to me. If it hadn't been for that, I never would have been able to take my family out to eat. He brought a great deal of joy to us."

Lambert's has attracted its share of celebrities. Conway Twitty, James Arness, Amanda Blake, Elvis Presley, The World's Tallest Man, The World's Heaviest Man, Tammy Wynette, Stan Musial, Dennis Weaver and Clint Eastwood are just a few of the celebrities who have tasted the Lambert's Cafe delights.

Lambert's opened for business in a small building on South Main Street in Sikeston on March 13, 1942. Earl and Agnes Lambert had 14 cents between them and then borrowed $1,500 to start the cafe. The cafe consisted of five employees, a nine-stool counter and eight tables for seating.

The cafe later moved to a bigger location on April 20, 1981, then to its present-day spot in June 1988. In March 1994, Lambert's Cafe opened its second restaurant near Branson, Mo., along Highway 65 South, about 18 miles from Branson, in the southwest corner of Missouri.

Construction for a third Lambert's Cafe in Foley, Ala., began in November 1995, with a grand opening scheduled for the summer of 1996.

Lambert's Cafe turns on the ovens for their famous hot rolls from 9:15 a.m. to 9 p.m., usually without stopping, each day. Lambert's bakes about 520 dozen rolls per day for a grand total of 2,246,400 individual rolls a year. The rolls are 5 inches in diameter, and if a person were to lay them down side by side, it would amount to 177.27 miles of rolls - about the distance between Sikeston and St. Louis.

Lambert's also uses 107,250 servings of jelly and 21,600 44-ounce cans of sorghum molasses. Lambert's makes and pours 476,136 cups of coffee, along with 40,392 gallons of tea, a year. A total of 61,200 pounds of Arkansas okra are served each year, along with 40,800 pounds of white beans and 13,107 gallons of slaw.

Norman's favorite job is passing potatoes. In fact, let me explain something here: Not only does a customer get a regular meal at Lambert's, but all these other items are passed by hand by Norman and his help. I have literally been so full when I left Lambert's that I thought my stomach was going to explode.

Norman says he always looks forward to waking up each morning and coming to work.

"My job is passing the potatoes," he said. "That's what I enjoy doing most. I can say I never dread coming to work."

Not only do customers get treated to the best food, but they may hear the sounds of home-grown piano player Geneva Bolen or grab one of the colorful Lambert's balloons. The Lambert's walls are decorated with a variety of pictures. The Missouri mule pictures are favorites in the restaurants.

Norman's life has not been void of the ups and downs we all experience. Norman's son, Todd, was tragically killed in an automobile accident Jan. 29, 1984. In Todd's memory, the Lamberts built a beautifully landscaped garden, with long walkways and a large wooden gazebo, eight miles from Sikeston next to a covered bridge.

"Todd worked in and around the restaurant from age 12," Norman said. "It was a tragic loss for our family. Only time has been able to ease the pain of that loss."

Norman was asked over and over to expand the restaurant into other cities, but always chose to stay only in Sikeston. Because of the customer load and the fact he wanted to create some additional jobs and opportunities for his employees, he decided to embark on new territory near Branson and now, Foley.

Marilyn Beaird is a Lambert's waitress at the new location near Branson.

She has worked for Norman for 14 years and considers Norman like family.

"He's been so good to my family," said Marilyn. "He is just like his daddy was. Norman offered my husband, Wayne, a part-time job when he needed it, and my daughter, Lisa, throws rolls for us here. I can go to Norman and tell him anything. Working in his restaurant is like being in a big family."

Cindy Fodge has also worked at Lambert's in Sikeston for nearly 14 years as a waitress.

Cindy describes Norman as a wonderful overall person.

"He has a big heart of gold," she said. "He would do anything for anybody."

Virginia Kelso has worked at Lambert's for the past 12 years. She is also a waitress.

"Norman is just a wonderful man," she said. "He treats everybody equally and does so much for people. When a disabled person comes into the restaurant, he wants us to take care of them and take their ticket. This is one way he knows he is helping people. Norman is like one of us. I really believe that is why he has been so successful."

Kelso recalled one night that Norman drove by and saw a vehicle broken down in a Sikeston parking lot. Norman actually gave the people money to fix their vehicle and sent a carry-out of the delicious Lambert's food.

Another time, a local blind girl's seeing eye dog died. When Norman heard of it, he persuaded a few others to join him in getting the girl a new dog.

Kelso said Norman loves animals and cannot stand to see them neglected.

"Norman has helped buy food for the Humane Society for years," Kelso said.

If a family with several children comes into Lambert's, Norman will often pick up the ticket.

Norman Lambert is not only a winner professionally, but as a person. It would be a learning experience for many American executives to fly to the Cape Girardeau, Mo., airport, rent a car, and make the 30-mile trek to this "down-home" restaurant in the Bootheel of Missouri.

I believe that anyone visiting there would see how remarkably this man runs a successful business, but never forgets the less fortunate, the disabled or his friends.

To me, there is something to be said for people like Norman Lambert who put loyalty, tradition, friends and family above dollar signs.

"Life is a two-way street. A lot of people don't remember that."

- Nick Boddie on his philosophy of business and life

DAY 21

"We Believe in People"

When one enters the Boddie-Noell Enterprises headquarters in Rocky Mount, N.C., a sign reads, "We Believe in People."

It doesn't take long to realize the sign is not just for show. "Life is a two-way street," said Nick Boddie in his office. "A lot of people don't remember that."

Nick and his brother Mayo, the company's founders, are truly self-made successes, starting in the early 1960s from scratch. Today, Boddie-Noell operates 300 Hardee's restaurants and has more than 13,000 employees. Boddie-Noell is the second-biggest franchisee of the Rocky Mount-based Hardee's system, trailing only Flagstar of Spartanburg, S.C., which was once headed by Carolina Panthers owner Jerry Richardson.

Charles Odom is a prime example of the Boddies' commitment to people of all walks of life and races, not always common in parts of the Deep South. Odom, who is black, first came in contact with the Boddies when he took a job at the Carleton House in 1961.

Odom began by washing dishes, but when things became extra busy, he would offer his services in the kitchen. It was in the kitchen that Odom discovered his true love - cooking.

"Nick Boddie saw I was interested in cooking, and he called me aside and offered me a job cooking," said Odom. "He explained to me that a dishwasher could be found anywhere, but you couldn't find just anyone to get behind a stove and cook. He made me realize that life would be better for me in cooking."

Once Odom showed an interest in cooking, Mayo Boddie stepped in and offered to help. Mayo suggested that Odom attend a cooking school in Rhode Island.

"I learned a lot of things from some of the great chefs around the world," said Odom. "It was one of the greatest experiences of my life. When I came back, I was a new man, plus a different cook. I was taught how to prepare fancy parties and be creative."

Odom's life could have been totally opposite had the Boddies not believed in him.

"I was tempted by peers to go the wrong way in life," said Odom.

One night, a supposed friend even asked Odom to steal wine from the Carleton House, but Odom couldn't take from the Boddies.

"I always kept the straight and honest path," said Odom. "I also watched things Nick and Mayo did and learned from them. I wanted to be like them. At the age of 21 I bought my first house."

Today, Odom is a professional chef at the Carleton House, a motel-restaurant owned by the company. Odom's cooking is loved by visitors to the well-known restaurant throughout the Southeast. He has purchased his second lovely home and raised a beautiful family. Without the Boddies, none of this would have been possible. Odom could have been another disastrous statistic.

Richard Jenkins and Judy Elks are other examples of the Boddies' belief in people. Jenkins, who is retired today, rose all the way from being a Hardee's crew member at age 16 to president of the entire Boddie-Noell group. In many companies, a person who started where Jenkins did would have never climbed the corporate ladder, but not in Boddie-Noell.

Judy Elks has been the personal secretary for the Boddies for the past 16 years. She probably knows more about Nick and Mayo than any-one other than their wives.

She rates Nick and Mayo the tops as far as bosses, as executives and friends.

"They have people's interests in their minds at all times. Neither Nick or Mayo have slowed down that much, even today. They believe leadership starts at the top. They also believe that, if you believe in people, there will be a chain-reaction of success that filters all the way down the organization.

"They want to do things for the community and people, but they don't want or need recognition," Elks said. "There are so many things they have done for people behind the scenes. I have loved my years of working with them."

Entering the office of someone like Nick Boddie, one might expect him to be dressed in a suit and tie.

Guess again.

"We got rid of the suits and ties several years ago," said Nick, looking relaxed and dressed in a plaid shirt, tan pants and tennis shoes, in one of my visits to Boddie-Noell.

Nick and Mayo, founders of Boddie-Noell Enterprises, have been bestowed with numerous honors in their careers. They have been East Carolina Council, Boy Scouts of America, Distinguished Citizens; they have been Distinguished Citizens of the Year, as named by the Rocky Mount Chamber of Commerce. Nick has been awarded the Distinguished Eagle Award by the Boy Scouts of America.

Believe it or not, Nick started his working career at the age of 10 by delivering the local Rocky Mount newspaper, *The Evening Telegram.* "I started out as a substitute carrier at 15 cents a day and then went to 20 cents," Nick recalled, going on to tell how much delivering newspapers taught him about the working world.

Wal-Mart founder Sam Walton, before his death, was known for dropping by his stores at odd times and doing a personal checklist. Nick and Mayo apply the same tactic with their restaurants.

"We spot-check businesses all the time," Nick said. "I have walked into some restaurants with a hat and sunglasses on. I try to look at things from a customer's point of view when I go in, looking at the parking lot first, then the restrooms, then the service."

"The Boddies are just unusually special," Charles Odom said. "They are down-to-earth and treat their employees with a lot of respect and help them in every way."

The professional Boddie is almost larger than life. But the private side of the Boddies is even greater.

Nick says, "I feel sorry for people without children. Family is what it is all about."

Several of Nick and Mayo's family members are involved in the Boddie-Noell business, which makes the corporation even more special.

It's obvious to me that Rocky Mount has been extremely lucky to have the Boddies in the community.

Nick and Mayo have a similar love affair with the eastern North Carolina city dubbed "The City on the Rise."

"We enjoy living in Rocky Mount. We're glad our ancestors settled in this neck of the woods," they both told me.

Anytime I needed to talk about my newspaper business I was planning, Nick and Mayo were there; all I had to do was ask. Once the paper started, anytime I called, Nick or Mayo were always there to talk. The first time I met with the two of them, I couldn't believe they would actually take time for someone like me.

Each time I called and set up an appointment, they took the time to listen to my ideas and go over my business plans. Once, when things got really tough in my business, both Nick and Mayo spent an hour with two associates and me. The brothers listened to our problems and tried to provide advice.

I don't know if either one of them knew how much that meant to me, but I will always remember that gift of time. The Boddies taught me, in that moment, you are never too big or too good to sit and listen to someone in need.

Nick and Mayo have been like guardian angels to many people in Rocky Mount over and over again.

The employees of Boddie-Noell Enterprises all love working with the Boddies. The loyalty they show to Nick and Mayo is returned many times over by them; perhaps this is why the company is successful. I knew several Boddie-Noell employees and not one time have I ever heard one say a bad thing about either brother.

I discovered over the years that many people who have acquired wealth and status often forget their roots, forget where they came from and instead, act as if their past means nothing to them.

Nick and Mayo Boddie have not forgotten what is really important in life, even though they have acquired plenty of wealth over the years through one small investment in a fledgling hamburger chain.

Basically, they have not forgotten where they came from or how to be humble. If there were ever men in this community to emulate, I think I discovered them.

My last talk with the Boddies closed with a peek outside the back window. Nick and Mayo gave me a glimpse of the company's planned future expansion.

The site was awesome. What was even more incredible was what the facility would mean for the employees of Boddie-Noell.

Stepping down the stairs, I saw the company slogan again, and thought that this is one sign that has real meaning. The Boddies, unlike many in business today, mean what they say.

I thought to myself, "If I could only be half of what Nick and Mayo Boddie have been during the course of their lives to their business, family and community, I'd really be something."

Nick and Mayo Boddie have material wealth, but they are also rich in the most important place - the heart.

"They told me with desire comes motivation. With motivation comes work. With the work comes results."

- Billy Mills on what motivated him in his life

DAY 22

A Platform for Good

The year is 1975. The place is a small history classroom in southwestern Illinois. Being shown to the high school track team is a two-minute clip of Billy Mills' 10,000-meter Tokyo Olympics victory 11 years earlier.

I was present in that classroom and one of the countless track athletes influenced by Mills' remarkable performance that October day in 1964. Twenty-eight years later, I was fortunate to spend an hour with my long-time hero.

******

Billy Mills remains a household name among sports fans today, years after his 1964 gold medal win in the Tokyo Olympics.

Many athletes forget to give back some of the good fortune that they have received, but not Mills.

Mills himself has helped raise millions of dollars to assist his Indian heritage. He is national chairman for Running Strong for American Indian Youth, a project of Christian Relief Services.

The former Olympian has spoken to countless children and adult groups throughout the country, promoting Christian values and providing inspiration.

Mills' story was the subject of a Walt Disney movie in the mid-1980s entitled *Running Brave*, which starred Robby Benson as Mills. I have always adored Billy Mills; the movie is one of my personal favorites, and each time I watch it, I have to fight back tears. I am very proud of what he has achieved in his life and the example he has set for others.

Mills received rave reviews for appearances when he was in Rocky Mount, N.C., as the special guest surrounding the 10th running of the annual Chase of Champions road race.

I will never forget my hour meeting with Billy Mills in his hotel room. When I extended my hand to greet him, my heart was pounding so loud, I was afraid he could hear it. This meeting ranks as one of the greatest moments of my life.

Mills was very easy to converse with in my interview with him. He greeted me with a warm, friendly smile. Immediately, I was at ease in the presence of this distance-running great.

Mills' memory of the fine details of the 1964 Olympics and his career is amazing. The track star was born on a Sioux reservation in South Dakota, losing his mother at age 7 and father at age 12.

"My older sister, Margie, basically became my mother and my older brother, Sid, became my father," Mills told me. "These two were extremely influential in my life."

Mills vividly remembers something a high school coach and his father told him about why he should work hard.

"They told me with desire comes motivation," Mills said. "With motivation comes work. With the work comes results.

"My dad then said, 'Billy, find a desire in your life. Learn how to speak English and compete against the white American. By doing that, you can take more of our culture into another generation.'"

Mills was ahead of his time, especially with his approach to speedwork. "I used to do about two miles and sprint no more than 150 yards, but sprint as fast as I could run without losing my composure," he said. "Years later, they discovered if you want to become fast, you run 20-25 seconds (for those 150 yards).

After 22 seconds, you go into oxygen debt.

"Without knowing it, I was ahead of my time."

Mills loves coming to races like the Chase of Champions, which benefits the Rocky Mount Family YMCA's Adaptive Swim Program for handicapped children. "The four sponsors of the event (four local businesses) are able to do something collectively to help all runners," Mills said. "The height of all competition is realizing that the ultimate competition is against oneself."

Mills does not believe in just reaping benefits from his God-given talents. Through the years, he has given so much in return.

"The greatest fault of the free enterprise system is profit at all costs," Mills told me. "Helping a multitude of people excites me. The sponsors of the race show that by helping put on this competition and collecting for the Adaptive Swim Program. That is a beautiful sharing aspect we need more of."

His willingness to share was evident to the race's coordinator, Allen Hinnant. "Billy Mills did more to promote our race than any of the guest runners we've had over the years," he said. "He visited several people throughout the community and took a lot of time for everyone. We loved having him here."

During our interview, I was spellbound by his presence. It was a day I will treasure for a long time.

I was able to reflect on the days in that history classroom in Illinois, watching over and over the clip of Billy Mills winning the 10,000 meters at the 1964 Tokyo Olympics.

Our school had a student body of only 400, so resources were tight. The projector was old and the screen was dingy, but I will never forget the images and inspiration Mills provided with his ferocious kick to bring home the gold medal for the USA.

I can remember hoping then that I could be just half as good as Billy Mills in track.

Nearly 20 years later, I feel the same way, except now not only as a runner, but as a person.

Society needs more giving, down-to-earth superstars like the man who hails from the Pine Ridge Reservation in South Dakota.

DAY 23
Fighting a Boo-Boo

A meeting with a blonde-haired, blue-eyed girl in 1995 opened my eyes as to how far we have come with leukemia research.

Amber Langston is the 3-year-old daughter of Bruce and Wendy Langston, and when I talked to her, she was waging a fight I hope and pray she will win against Acute Lymphocytic Leukemia, or ALL.

Bruce said when Amber was first diagnosed, it was an extremely difficult time.

"My wife, Wendy, had a really hard time sleeping after the diagnosis," he said. "She was very distraught. I've always been the type that can handle extenuating circumstances. I had a knowledge about leukemia because of my work as an occupational therapy assistant, so from the start I thought she had an excellent chance at surviving."

Bruce did not have hospital insurance at the time Amber was diagnosed with her illness. He said Amber had been on a cancer policy with his mother, but his mother was in the process of changing plans.

"There was a three-week layover in the policies," said Bruce. "She asked me if I wanted to continue the present policy until the other one was in effect, and like a dummy, I discontinued it."

Bruce said that he simply couldn't afford health insurance at the time Amber got sick.

"We planned to get it soon," he said. "We had so many bills. I learned some valuable lessons. You should always have health insurance for your family, no matter what. It should be your top priority."

Her survival chances are very good, thanks to modern treatment methods. In fact, she has a 75-90 percent chance of pushing the disease into remission.

One look at her will tell you that she is a sweet, innocent and lovable child. She, in no way, looks like a person who is battling cancer, except for an incision in her chest area that she showed me.

Bruce said Amber was the typical 2- and 3-year-old before she got sick.

"She was feisty, fun-loving and energetic," Bruce said. "When she got sick, she could barely walk and had no energy. Today, Amber is again full of energy, boisterous, but loves to look pretty in her dresses. She always has a kiss and hug for her mommy and daddy. She is as sweet as she can be. Amber is almost always smiling and happy."

ALL, as I learned, is considered the most curable form of leukemia in children. It represents 85 percent of all forms of the disease in persons under 21. It attacks primarily those between the ages of 2-10, and the overall rate of attack is 1.1 persons per 100,000 population. More than 2,000 people will be diagnosed with ALL this year.

Thirty years ago, ALL patients usually lived for only a few months after they were diagnosed. There have been unbelievable advances in treating the disease, particularly in the last 10 years. Today, 95 percent of all patients go into remission, and 50-75 percent of these patients live for five years or longer, with a potential cure rate in excess of 50 percent for children.

The typical ALL treatment consists of drugs to battle the disease, with dosage levels adjusted to meet individual needs.

People in the Seneca area did not let the Langstons struggle with their problems alone. In fact, the area sent countless donations to the Langstons and even put on a benefit concert that raised about $3,700 to defray Amber's medical expenses.

Lila Doyle Nursing Home even feeds Amber's father, Bruce, for free each day in their cafeteria.

The Greenville Children's Miracle Network named Amber its poster child for 1996, which was probably the greatest single financial benefit to the Langstons.

"This has defrayed most of our medical expenses," Bruce told me. "Our bills had gotten over the $100,000 mark, but the Children's Miracle Network helped with about $70,000-$80,000 of the bills."

Bruce and Wendy have both changed their outlook on life since Amber developed leukemia. In fact, it is likely both will work in the fund-raising area for cancer research for many years to come.

"I think Wendy and I both look at things more realistically as to what's important in life," said Bruce. "We still get upset about things, but now it takes a lot more to get us upset."

The first time I met Amber, I was extremely captivated by her. In fact, everyone in our newspaper office fell in love with her.

I'll never forget what she said when she looked at me with her beautiful, angelic blue eyes and referring to her leukemia said, "We've got to fight this boo-boo. We've got to fight this boo-boo."

Amber and her family appear to have won the fight against her boo-boo. In early April 1996, after six months of agonizing treatment and therapy, Amber entered the patient management stage with her cancer.

"Her bone marrow is clear and the cancer is in remission," said Bruce. "Twenty years ago, people died from even a simple type of leukemia. Without the miracle of modern-day medicine and technology, Amber would be an angel in heaven right now. Instead, she is an angel right here in our arms."

TODAY'S QUOTE:

"...you plant the seeds, nurture the growth and wait for the bounty."
**- The educational philosophy of Dean Bare, an administrator
at a Daughters of the American Revolution school in South Carolina**

DAY 24

Honesty is the Best Policy

A question for you:

If you walked into, say, Wal-Mart and discovered a $100 bill, would you return it to store management?

I would hope the answer to this question would be yes.

Wesley, just 12 years old and a student at Tamassee DAR School in Tamassee, S.C., was faced with exactly that situation at his hometown Wal-Mart during a shopping trip (we're not printing his full name to protect his privacy).

Wesley had been out doing shopping with fellow students and his parents when he came upon a $100 bill in the greeting area.

I'm willing to bet his eyes popped out of his head when he saw the money; after all, how many 12-year-olds ever even *think* about seeing a $100 bill?

But the youngster did not buckle under to the internal urge to pocket the bill and buy himself video games or baseball cards or even a Carolina Panthers NFL jersey.

Instead, he picked up the bill and took it to a Wal-Mart employee. The man who had lost the money was still in the store and was telling store officials about his loss. He was so thankful when the money was returned, he presented the boy with a reward. Wal-Mart didn't forget, either; the store presented Wesley with a gift certificate.

Now, lest you think Wesley comes from an environment of spoiled rich kids, let me explain that his school is attended by disadvantaged or abandoned youngsters. One of the things the school, funded by the Daughters of the American Revolution, tries to do is instill a solid moral fiber into the students who attend.

The school was founded many years ago in a mountain village of the Cherokee Indians, where a famous fire prophet lived, according to legend. The prophet's great wisdom and power of healing were attributed to the possession of an unusually large ruby. With their gift of picturesque speech, the Indians called the glowing ball of fire "The Sunlight God."

People came from far and wide to consult with the prophet. At his death, the Indians obeyed his parting instructions and buried him with the stone he clasped in his breast. The knoll, where the grave lay, was called "Tamassee, the Place of the Sunlight God." Today, boys and girls from several states and the surrounding communities come to this school.

Dean Bare, the school's administrator, said he was overjoyed to learn how Wesley responded to finding the money. He told me of a *Reader's Digest* experiment where dropped wallets were placed in buildings and malls in cities across the nation and the reactions of people who encountered the wallets were observed.

Bare believes the business he is in is a lot like planting a crop; you plant the seeds, nurture the growth, then wait to see the bounty.

In Wesley's case, the seeds have been planted and are in the process of germinating. It was very fortunate for the man who lost the $100 in Wal-Mart that day that Wesley had the honesty and resourcefulness to return it.

TODAY'S QUOTE:

"It is something people go by every day and don't see. You
don't understand that until you come out."

- Dan Davis on the homeless shelter in Rocky Mount, N.C.

DAY 25
It's Not What You Think

For several years when I lived in Rocky Mount, N.C., I drove along Franklin Street every day and never noticed the Rocky Mount Community Shelter.

The shelter's director then, Dan Davis, said that I was no different than the majority of the people in Rocky Mount.

"It is really something people go by every day and don't see," Davis said. "You don't understand that until you come out. Most people expect to find something entirely different. We really want people to see what we are doing and understand that these are real people we are working with."

One night, I took up Davis' offer to pay the shelter a visit, and it opened my eyes to the situation with the homeless in Rocky Mount.

What did I expect?

Well, truthfully, I expected to meet inarticulate, unkempt people - quite to the contrary of what I saw.

Val Stovall, who was client activities coordinator for the shelter that night, greeted me near the door. "You must be Dan," he said.

"Yeah, I'm Dan."

"You don't looked dressed to work in the kitchen," he joked.

After a tour of the kitchen, Stovall and I began talking about the shelter and many of the things going on there.

Stovall was a bundle of energy that night. "I find it rewarding just being here," he said. "Our entire staff is good. We have good days and bad days, but most of the time, they are satisfying."

After I talked to him, I settled into the environment to chat with some of the residents. At that point, I met Denise, who was at the shelter battling a drug addiction. She was seated with a few friends in the dining area finishing her meal.

"It has been an inspiration to be here," she told me. "I was here once before. I have had a lot of support since I've been here. I've never seen them turn anyone away.

"I thank God for the shelter."

Denise said she was hoping to get her life back on track. "I want to go back to school and counsel women who are abused," she said. "I'm really looking forward to Christmas. This will be my first real Christmas."

One of the things I wanted to know was just what it was like to be homeless.

Leslie, a 24-year-old man seated nearby explained, "It is basically a very lonely feeling. It is not a good thing to experience in a lifetime.

"We do have a nice family type of thing going here. Everyone gets along. I plan on getting my life situated soon and would like to get a job at a supermarket."

After visiting with Leslie, I sat down for what became a lengthy visit with Leon, 26.

Leon was most interesting to chat with, which is not surprising, considering his background. He spent three years at North Carolina A&T in Greensboro majoring in mechanical engineering. At the present time, he was working as a welder in Rocky Mount.

"I've had misfortune," he said. "I have been here about two weeks. I think if something bad happened to somebody, this would be a very good place to regroup. The staff is very helpful.

"They keep it very clean here. The shelter helps in so many ways. You can even work on getting your GED here. The people who come here are really very good people."

Our conversation was distracted by a youth group from Sunset Avenue Baptist Church. The girls brought gloves, hats and Bibles to the homeless men and women. The sincerity was most apparent in the eyes of these young people.

Minutes later, a choral ensemble from South Rocky Mount Church of God came to perform. "They come pretty regularly," Davis told me. "They perform about six times a year. The churches help us so much; they provide about 35 percent of our funding and also volunteering."

"The people who donate are so generous," Leon said. "People come here for a variety of reasons, but homelessness happens every day. From being here, it has shown me the people of Rocky Mount do care."

The kitchen was my next stop on the visit. I talked to two young men performing community service penalties. Both admitted it was a good experience.

"I just like helping people," Scott said. "You get to see so many different things here. Last night, we just about had to deliver a baby."

I walked into the dining room with a new perspective. I thought that these people are not very different from me.

Despite a difference in material possessions and providence, they are just like everybody else. They deserve a chance just as much as the next person.

Leon said to me, "Dan, I'm glad you came here. A lot of people don't know about the shelter and I think they have the wrong impression."

Climbing back into my car, I felt sad and a bit sick to my stomach.

Suddenly, my bills and day-to-day work pressures seemed inconsequential. "I am so lucky to have what I have," I told myself.

I drove down Franklin Street, determined to tell the shelter's story to everyone in town.

"I was absolutely devastated... I had always wanted to help people as a nurse. Fortunately, the hospital was very supportive and did what it could during my battles (with a brain tumor)."

- Cindy Floyd on her feelings after learning she had a brain tumor

DAY 26
Getting Educated

Questions, questions and more questions.

In a given day, Cindy Floyd fields 15-20 phone calls with a multitude of diabetes questions to her Oconee Memorial Hospital office in Seneca, S.C. After hours, she often accepts many calls at home. In seconds, she must formulate a response and know where to send the patient if she cannot satisfy their needs.

Cindy never really intended to become a diabetes educator, but because of some near-fatal setbacks, setbacks that eventually cost her the vision in one eye, Floyd was forced to give up her position as third-shift supervisor of nursing.

However, in her current position as an educator, she is in a much better position to touch more lives than perhaps she ever could if she had remained a nursing supervisor.

"It can be very stressful," said Cindy. "You have to get information back quickly to the patients. I cannot give prescriptions to patients; that is where the doctor comes in. I guess as a young nurse I could have never envisioned I would be doing what I am doing. Now I see so many needs of patients with diabetes and other chronic diseases. The key is setting long-term goals to avoid long-term complications. When the disease process is long-term, it can't be solved in one session.

"In the beginning, most diabetes patients are overwhelmed. Many start with complications because they are overweight. A good rule I apply is to treat every one else the way I want to be treated. I always ask myself, 'Is this how I would want my daddy treated?'"

Cindy has been an unbelievable help to me in my battle with diabetes. I have called her over and over with quick questions. She always has an answer or guides me in the proper direction to get the answer. What has impressed me most is that she always takes time for the patient, no matter what time of day, or no matter what she is doing.

Cindy even talked me into seeking special treatment in Atlanta for my illness. After several visits to Atlanta, I am on a new program of four insulin injections a day, mixed with constant glucose testing. Cindy has probably added a decade or more to my life with her advice. I cannot imagine how many others she has influenced the same way.

Cindy's own physical problems began in 1983. While pregnant with her first child, Cindy began to notice she was having vision problems, accompanied by a series of headaches.

These problems persisted and eventually worsened, causing Cindy to seek help. She had a series of CAT scans done, and the results were, to say the least, frightening.

Cindy had a brain tumor - attached to the optic nerve in her left eye.

Nothing could be done to the tumor while she was pregnant; a biopsy showed the tumor to be benign, but that was all that could be done.

Cindy's daughter was born in March 1984; by January 1985, Cindy found herself in a hospital room in Pittsburgh, taking treatments for the tumor.

Surgeons soon found they could not remove the tumor because it was attached to her optic nerve. A plate was later inserted into her skull, and radiation treatments quickly began.

While she was in the hospital, she encountered several less-than-ideal situations. One time, a nurse carelessly ripped a tube off of her, taking some skin with it. The hospital also ran the wrong tests on her several times.

After treatments, Cindy returned home and attempted to resume a normal life. A year and a half later, Cindy's second daughter was born, but an MRI scan found the tumor had grown larger, and she was forced to go back to the hospital (this time, in another city closer to home) to battle the tumor again.

All the treatments and associated problems with the tumor cost Cindy dearly. She lost all vision in her left eye and 20 percent upper-right peripheral vision in her right eye.

All of the problems forced Cindy to give up her position as supervisor.

"I was absolutely devastated," she told me. "I had always wanted to help people as a nurse. Fortunately, the hospital was very supportive and helped me in every way they could during my battles."

Eventually, a position for a patient educator for diabetes opened, and Cindy applied for it. She was immediately hired, and in 1991, became a certified diabetes educator.

The problems she has encountered with her eyesight have helped her empathize with people with diabetes. She is now quicker to notice potential problems that people with diabetes may encounter, especially with their vision.

Helping people is one of the greatest things anyone can do. Cindy Floyd is thankful that she can still help someone every day.

"Dogs are much like humans - the more they know someone cares, the chances at survival are that much better."

- A University of Georgia veterinarian in charge of Tiffany, a miniature poodle stricken with diabetes

DAY 27
Something in Common

When pets become deathly sick, many owners decide the time and effort to nurse the animal back to health isn't worth it.

James and Judy Hopkins of Seneca, S.C., faced this decision in April 1992 when their miniature poodle, Tiffany, was diagnosed with diabetes.

Most people would have put the pet to sleep or given it away, deciding that the effort to keep her healthy wouldn't be feasible.

The Hopkins thought otherwise and decided not to give up on Tiffany; instead they sent their pet to the University of Georgia's School of Veterinary Medicine Teaching Hospital in Athens, Ga., and visited her nearly every other day for two weeks.

After Tiffany was diagnosed with diabetes, the Hopkins were told that Tiffany might not survive the first night, but the doctor in charge of her case also reminded them that dogs are much like humans - the more they know someone cares, the chances of survival are that much better.

Tiffany had many of the same symptoms that humans with diabetes exhibit, such as vomiting and an excessive thirst. When she went to UGA, she was one sick little dog; a blood-sugar test revealed that her level was a shockingly high 480.

Tiffany had come to the Hopkins family one year after their son, Jeff, had departed to attend nearby Clemson University. She was a Christmas present to Judy to ease the void Judy had been feeling, and grew to be part of the family so quickly that the couple decided to purchase a tiny casket to bury Tiffany in their yard should something ever happen to her.

After some fantastic care from the people at the UGA clinic and some tender loving care from her owners, Tiffany eventually went home.

At this point, Tiffany entered the new, strange world of diabetes, which is a disease in which the absence of insulin, a vital hormone, causes the body to improperly process the blood's sugars.

Like humans with diabetes, Tiffany had to be placed on a restricted diet, given two injections of insulin a day and given an exercise routine to follow.

The Hopkins had to come up with a special mixture of food for her to eat each day and administer the two injections. Like humans, the injections weren't something Tiffany looked forward to; in fact, James said that Tiffany took off running when it came time for the injections.

Fortunately, the shots were soon accepted as a regular part of the routine and now Tiffany even comes quickly to James when she hears him rattle the insulin syringes. James believes Tiffany feels better after each shot and realizes that it is part of her survival.

Now, before you start thinking that canine diabetes is rare, Type I, or insulin-dependent, diabetes is much more common than you think. One in about every 200 dogs in America has diabetes, with female dogs getting it twice as often as male dogs, said Linda Fulton, who is a clinical veterinarian at Clemson University.

"The incidence of diabetes in miniature poodles, dachshunds, schnauzers, Cairn terriers and beagles, especially, is on the rise in the United States," Fulton said.

While the Hopkins have the main responsibility to take care of Tiffany, they aren't without help. Judy's parents, Mr. and Mrs. Ervin

Lee, join in the caretaking by watching Tiffany during the week while James and Judy are at work. Clarence Towe, a friend who by day is the superintendent of operations for the School District of Oconee County (S.C.), also gets involved by helping to administer injections when James and Judy aren't around.

There are many mornings when one can find James looking for drops of Tiffany's urine to test on ketone strips. He is willing to bet more than one person thinks he has lost his mind when they see him trying to chase down his pet's urine for a test.

Both of them say Tiffany, in some ways, is like a child with diabetes, but to the casual observer, no one would realize there is anything physically wrong with her.

And yet, despite all the problems she has presented, Tiffany has also brought plenty of joy to the Hopkins.

"I just can't tell you how much she has meant to us," Judy said. "We are so glad to have her. She's my baby."

One thing I have never understood is why people do not stick with their pets through thick and thin. I have a lot of admiration for the Hopkins and what they have done to keep their pet healthy.

And I have something in common with Tiffany - I, too, have diabetes.

That's enough for me to feel a real kinship with this pooch.

DAY 28

The Good Samaritan

Good Samaritans are not easy to be found today.

Often, people pass by difficult situations where another person is in need because they might worry about personal safety. That is certainly understandable, considering the way our society is today.

Melanie Dawson, who lives in Mountain Rest, S.C., could have by-passed a life-threatening situation she encountered one day. She had been following a disoriented driver traveling through the mountains of Upstate South Carolina. Several things were going through her mind. She was worried, for instance, that the person she was following was on drugs or was drunk.

"I just kept praying that somehow, I could get him to stop," she recalled.

Disregarding her personal safety, she darted in front of the driver and forced him to pull over. When Melanie got to the driver, she found him dazed and confused.

She asked him for his car keys, and thankfully, he obliged. At that point, Melanie still wasn't sure if the person she was dealing with was on drugs or drunk - until the driver finally mumbled that he had diabetes.

At that point, Melanie knew the person was in big trouble.

With his keys in hand, Melanie quickly went to a local convenience store and called for help. She was told to offer the person orange juice to raise his blood-sugar level.

A few sips of juice later, the person's blood sugar went back to normal and he snapped out of the dream-like state.

It so happened that when the person with diabetes had left his office that day, he had forgotten his lunch and worked out heavily at a local health club.

The workout caused his sugar level to drop to a dangerous level, throwing him into shock after he had gotten into his truck to go back to work.

Melanie asked the person to go with her to the store and eat a sandwich. She stayed with him until he was totally out of danger.

"I guess I just like to help people," she told the man.

It was very fortunate that Melanie had seen the developing situation. If she had not stopped the person, he could very well have gone into a diabetic coma, losing all consciousness. He could have easily driven off the side of a mountain road and down a cliff or hit another vehicle, killing himself or someone else.

In fact, the man drove right around a dangerous spot called "Dead Man's Curve." Only a miracle could have prevented him from going off the cliff into the rocks several hundred feet below.

This incident sparked me to look up the Biblical tale of the Good Samaritan, which is found in Luke 10:30-37.

The story goes like this:

A man was making his way from Jerusalem to Jericho one day when he encountered a group of thieves, who stripped him, beat him and wounded him, leaving him on the road half-dead. A priest and a Levite saw him, but refused to offer assistance.

Then a Samaritan journeying by, saw the injured man and had compassion for him. He bound the wounds, pouring in oil and wine and helped him to an inn, where he took care of the person.

This parable is something I believe in; when a person is in need, we should show compassion and give him or her a hand.

Sure, there is always a risk. The Samaritan in the Biblical story had plenty to risk; there were major differences between Samaritans and Jews, and the Samaritan risked persecution from his own people for helping a Jew.

Melanie herself may have met a drug addict or worse when she stopped the car. Instead, she found a person with diabetes who needed her help desperately.

Without Melanie's courage and compassion, that man could have been badly injured or even killed, as well as someone in his path.

I should know. I'm the person for whom Melanie took that chance and saved.

AUTHOR'S NOTE: Nearly a year after the incident, Melanie stopped by the newspaper office where I work and asked me if I remembered her. I didn't at first, but after she reminded me of the incident, I couldn't believe she stopped by to see me. I gave her a big hug.

She told me some interesting things. First, she mentioned that she had been traveling the opposite direction from me on the mountain road that day and did a complete turnaround in order to follow me.

Then, she told me that her grandmother had diabetes, so she knew what to do when I muttered out that I had the disease. Otherwise, she admitted, she probably would not have known what to do to help me.

It was very fortunate timing that Melanie saw me and then knew what to do to help.

If there is such a thing as an angel on earth, Melanie Dawson would be that for me. It sure seems more than a coincidence that Melanie is the one who stopped and saved me. My guardian angels had to have been involved, working through her.

I've asked myself over and over, how many people in today's society would have risked their personal safety to help a weaving rural driver in need? I owe Melanie a lot more than the simple lunch I bought her after we reunited.

"As you walk in (Collins), you have this wonderful feeling of peace and love, which I know is there. The main thing here which Anne was telling me, is that Christianity comes into all, and I think that is wonderful."

- Countess Jeanne-Marie Dickens of North Yorkshire in Great Britain, during her visit to the Collins Children's Home

DAY 29
People Who Truly Care

Christmas time is a time of giving, sharing and thinking of children, especially those who live in the Collins Children's Home in Seneca, S.C.

In fact, if it weren't for the December contributions, says home co-founder Anne Rackley, "we wouldn't make it."

"During Christmas, we get sponsors for our children," Anne said. "They help with gifts and play Santa Claus. If these people didn't sponsor the children and give gifts, we wouldn't be able to afford nice Christmas gifts for the children.

"We get help from businesses, civic clubs, church groups and Sunday schools. It really is a special time of the year."

Warren Detrick of Seneca, a volunteer for the home, has been friends with Anne for more than 13 years after a chance encounter at Clemson University. One day, while Anne was working as an office supervisor at the university, a thunderstorm hit and Warren was in the vicinity of her office.

Normally, Rackley would not have been in the front office but was seated there at the time, assisting someone else. Detrick, seeking refuge from the storm, wound up talking about the home with Rackley for more than an hour. Learning that Detrick collected antique toys, Rackley knew that his love of toys was a good match for her love of children.

Detrick has been committed to the home ever since, serving in various board and volunteer capacities.

Detrick has entertained children and done magic and toy presentations at his home for most of these 13 years. This past year, lunch was catered by the Winn-Dixie supermarket in Walhalla, S.C. The manager of the store, Larry White, and the pharmacy manager, Harold Alexander, demonstrated their compassion for the kids by arranging for the luncheon and the gifts.

The children were beautifully dressed when they arrived at the Detrick home. Detrick performed his magic and toy shows for the children with much enthusiasm and love for the children.

"Warren has meant so much to the home," Anne said. "He has helped in all phases and gets personally involved."

Another person who has been involved since the start of the home in 1980 is Wayne Gallimore, who has served as chairman of the Collins Home board for several years. Gallimore was even involved with the home in an advisory capacity before it officially opened in 1980.

"Kids are so often overlooked," said Gallimore, who works not only with the Collins Home but also with area Boy Scouts. "Many of the kids at the home are products of failed families. We see so much of that today throughout the country."

Gallimore remembers many different things about the home through the years, but watching two children come in who were physically, sexually and emotionally abused has stayed with him.

"The children's father did everything bad you can imagine to the children," Gallimore said. "The mother had also been abused. To see the children begin to have some semblance of a life and go to bed knowing they weren't going to be attacked is an incredible feeling.

"It's that kind of thing you see at the Collins Home. It can be very frustrating and very difficult emotionally being involved, but it is great when you see positive results. When you see three or four children from the family stay together and see the parents improve, it really makes you feel good. It gives you a warm, fuzzy feeling."

Another person whom Anne describes as an angel to the home was Seneca's Melvin Golden, who died of cancer April 13, 1996.

"He was a simple, nice, quiet man," Anne said. "Once a month, he would pull up in his pickup truck, and all the kids would run to the truck to see what he had brought. He always had fruit, vegetables, cake mix, sugar, crackers and whatever else he could come up with.

"He had been sick, and I know at times, he could hardly come out. But he came faithfully each month. The last time I saw Melvin, he was delivering food and supplies to the Collins Home on a Saturday afternoon. He appeared to feel reasonably well, but I knew he was determined to be brave. Melvin Golden was a brave man. Battling cancer did not slow him down often.

"He never let his own misfortune get in the way of being kind to others. Because his motivation to help others came from a genuine love for the Lord, Melvin Golden did not expect any praise or credit for what he did - he would barely give us a chance to say, 'Thank you.'"

Anne recalled one November when Golden asked her if she had enough sponsors for her children's Christmas presents. She told him "no." He asked if she would give him five children to sponsor and not to worry about them.

Three weeks later, he came back and had all the sponsors for the gifts, and told her if she needed more, he would find them.

Every family needs a loving grandpa. Thanks to the angelic spirit of "Grandpa" Niles Workman, the Collins Kids have the best.

Approaching the Rackleys in 1984 with a genuine desire to help the home, Niles was quickly put to work as a volunteer. Then, as a board member, he organized the successful annual chicken barbecue fund-raiser and continues to assist in fund raising.

Workman says knowing and loving these special children and their families makes his efforts easy. He likes the reward for hard work - hugs from his "grandchildren."

A civic group which is deeply involved with the Collins Home and the lives of the children is the Cosmopolitan Women's Club. Cosmopolitan club members have shown many times that they have a soft place in their hearts for the children. The club, founded in 1987 by Lucille Groves of Seneca, has used that kind spirit to put on an annual fashion show and luncheon for the home. The idea of the show came up when the club was formed, and it has not only become one of the home's biggest fund-raisers, but one of the most anticipated events in the area each year.

The spirit that embraces the Collins Home is not limited to Upstate South Carolina, however; its work has become known internationally, as well. The most famous Collins Home visit came last year near Thanksgiving when Countess Jeanne-Marie Dickens of North Yorkshire in Great Britain and married to Charles Dickens' great, great grandson, Christopher Charles, toured. Charles Dickens is the world-famous novelist, author of *Great Expectations*, *A Tale of Two Cities* and *A Mutual Friend*.

Countess Dickens and Anne Rackley met through a similar interest in life - a love for Department 56 lighted houses. It is through the Department 56 Charles Dickens Signature Series that funds for the Charles Dickens Heritage Foundation are generated.

Countess Dickens was immediately taken by Anne Rackley and her enthusiasm for the home.

"She has such drive," said Countess Dickens. "Just looking at her and seeing that she was so neat herself and such an impressive person, I was drawn to her. I like supporting, with the foundation, people like her.

"As soon as you walk in (Collins), you have this wonderful feeling of peace and love, which I know is there," she said. "The main thing here which Anne was telling me, is that Christianity comes into all aspects of the home, and I think it is wonderful. "

After her initial visit at the home, the Charles Dickens Heritage Foundation donated $5,000 to the Collins Children Home for its future growth fund. This year alone, 150 children had to be turned away from the home because of lack of space.

"The next morning, Jeanne-Marie asked Joe and me to sit and talk to her," Anne recalled. "'I like what you are doing,' she said, 'and I want the foundation to be a part of it. We will take the $5,000 and add another $20,000 to sponsor a family room in your new home. My only request is that you put a framed portrait of Charles Dickens, which I will provide, and some of the little lighted houses in the room.'

"We (the Rackleys) checked to see how much it would be to sponsor a family room in the new home, and it turned out to be exactly $25,000. She (Countess Dickens) about leaped off the sofa when she heard that. 'I knew it, I knew it!,'" she exclaimed.

The Countess' visit educated the children from the standpoint of literature. It helped the children see the work of Charles Dickens through her eyes and made them feel truly unique.

The Countess herself was, at one time, a refugee and an orphan, but still made something of her life. One of the things that helped her have a love for America was an American soldier who gave her candies during World War II. She had to flee Hungary because of the war.

The Countess is such a lively person. You cannot help but love life when you are around her. She is determined get the best out of life. She is dedicated to give her best effort, as well.

The home is planning to expand its presence in the area. The project, known as the Community of Caring, will increase its care by 16 children, enhance family interaction through expanded parental counseling, implement independent living programs for older children and establish crisis care for short-term placements.

I hope the Rackleys and their supporters are able to expand the home into additional cottages and assist many other youngsters who desperately need a home.

People like Countess Jeanne-Marie Dickens, Detrick, Gallimore, Golden, Workman, Groves and the Rackleys help to make every day like Christmas at the Collins Children's Home and are everyday, angels.

"You have to remember that there are a lot more needy and desperate people out there, other than yourself."

- Adam Rumoshosky on why he donates volunteer time to many causes

DAY 30

Retired, But Not Retiring

April 19, 1995

Dear Adam:

How touched and delighted I am to hear from you across the years and miles! It is wonderful to know that you remain a champion for beauty. I believe it must be contagious working in that "vineyard"! My interest goes on and on, although the "long tooth of time" limits my ability to work effectively.

Now that the Wildflower Center's splendid new facilities have been completed, at 82, I am going to do what I have been trying for the last couple of years to accomplish - that is "retire" and have open windows of time to do whatever calls to my heart.

With appreciation and warmest thoughts of you and Marguerite,

Lady Bird Johnson

December 28, 1965

Dear Adam:

Just a brief note at year's end to thank you for your work in 1965 on behalf of the Discover America program. Your efforts are not only aiding your own industry, but are serving the national interest, as well. I believe you have good reason for gratification.

My best wishes for the year ahead.

Sincerely,

Hubert H. Humphrey

******

Next to his family and business career, most of Adam Rumoshosky's time, even in his retirement, has been devoted to public service.

He spent most of his business career in New York City with the American Petroleum Institute (from 1937-70), where he was director of its Marketing Division until he left to become foreign news editor of a daily oil trade paper published by McGraw-Hill (from 1970-79).

During his working career, he was a member of Lady Bird Johnson's National Beautification Committee for four years. The committee held meetings at the White House each month, with Mrs. Johnson presiding. Adam says he found Mrs. Johnson, wife of President Lyndon Johnson, to be "just about the finest person I've ever known." She mentions Adam's active role as a member of her committee in her book *A White House Diary.*

He was also a member of an industry group that organized the national anti-litter organization Keep America Beautiful, Inc. Similarly, he was a founding board member of Discover America, Inc., created by the travel industry to promote travel in the United States.

When he finally retired from McGraw-Hill in 1979, Rumoshosky was looking for a place away from the hustle and bustle of daily meetings, deadlines and big-city life. After a thorough search of the Southeast, Adam and his wife, Marguerite, elected to build their retirement home in Seneca, S.C.

Rumoshosky says retiring to Seneca has been a happy experience for him. He has made many new Southern friends who have accepted him warmly, calling him "one of the good Yankees," he reports with obvious pleasure.

In 1984, after living in Seneca for five years, he was given a surprise birthday party by eight of his new golfing buddies, who presented him with a gift inscribed "Happy 70th, Adam. Thank you for moving to Seneca. We know you could have moved anywhere." This gesture of friendship really touched him and truly made him feel right at home.

Not wanting to just lie around and do nothing, from the very beginning he became an active member of his new community, giving his time to many local causes. For example, he has been a member of the board of directors of the Greater Seneca Chamber of Commerce and the Friends of the Oconee County Library system (he wrote the official history of the system to commemorate its 40th anniversary). Also, he is a member and former president of the Seneca Koffee Club and has been a member of the Advisory Council of the UpCountry Seniors Golf Association.

At the UCSGA's annual luncheon in 1993, attended by more than 100 senior golfers, Adam became the first recipient of what has become the annual Dean Davis Award, memorializing a prominent deceased member. The award cited him as "an outstanding sportsman and for his service and devotion to the community and its citizens." His comment to me: "I was awed by this recognition, which I'll always treasure."

He also sails his 20-foot sloop on Lake Keowee, and for 12 years, he has been editor of a quarterly newsletter for Port Santorini, the Seneca subdivision where he lives.

Together with his wife Marguerite, he was a volunteer for three years at the Homework Center at Seneca's Northside Elementary School, receiving a special commendation from the State Superintendent of Education for "extraordinary service to the children of South Carolina."

The biggest cause he has worked with, however, is one he helped to get off the ground in his new hometown - the Keep Oconee Beautiful Association (KOBA), based on the Keep America Beautiful program. He was the founding chairman and has remained a KOBA board member and officer.

Since KOBA was founded, Rumoshosky has helped it become one of the most respected public action groups in the county. He and his group's efforts to keep Oconee County, S.C., and the Lake Keowee area in which he lives clean and beautiful has been taken to heart by many people in the area. The organization now boasts a dues-paying membership of around 500 families and 100 businesses, professional groups and civic clubs. Lady Bird Johnson, in fact, is an honorary member of the group.

In 1995, KOBA collected 41,000 pounds of trash on 143 miles of roadside throughout Oconee County. South Carolina Govs. Carroll Campbell and David Beasley recognized KOBA so many times for its efforts in keeping the area clean that KOBA now has been permanently installed in the South Carolina Hall of Fame for Community Improvement.

And it's not just the retirees who take part in the KOBA program, either. It's all sorts of people from Seneca, Clemson, Walhalla, Westminster, Fair Play and other towns included in this region.

Another time, Adam heard that the local Salvation Army was having a few problems raising money and getting volunteers during the annual Christmas bell-ringing campaign in Oconee County.

So he volunteered and managed to raise nearly $400 for the Army's efforts by donating 11-and-a-half hours of his time over the holiday season.

Thanks to Adam's efforts, many families in the area had a happier

Christmas season. The reason he did it, though, is a simple one: "You have to remember there are a lot more desperate and needy people out there, other than yourself," he told me.

There is no doubt that Adam Rumoshosky is a selfless man, a man who has made quite a difference in his community and the lives he has touched.

If only everyone out there could say that when they reach his age of 81 - and he was even going strong at his local blood bank until he had to have a pacemaker installed in April 1996.

But without a doubt, the most important part of his life, besides Marguerite, has been his children. A note to Adam commemorating Marguerite and his 50th wedding anniversary from his daughter, Jill, sums up what Adam means to her as a father.

True to the family's sense of humor, it went like this:

Dear Daddy,

Thank you so much for everything that you've done for me. I may just be a Jerky Kid, but I know that you must have done something right in raising me, as you apparently haven't found a good reason to disown me yet. Here are just some of the things that you have done for me that I consider to be very special:

• You built a little tunnel/playhouse for me in the woodpile up on the hill behind the house.

• You ran about 10 miles a day holding onto the seat of my first two-wheeler while teaching me how to ride. These days, they call that "aerobic interval training."

• You taught me, by your example, that I can be an honest person and still succeed in this world.

• You gave me your love of gardening.

• You gave me your last name. (Oops...I should move this one to the

"Negative" column.)

• *You provided me with the great role model for my business career. I have always considered you to be the epitome of an executive.*

• *You didn't teach me how to play golf. This has saved me much time, money and aggravation during my life.*

• *You played it totally cool when you drove me home after Tim's car accident. I was almost expecting to be locked in the trunk or dragged behind the car by a rope. Instead, you maintained a sense of humor that I find amazing to this day.*

• *You paid for my college and graduate education. The simplicity of this statement in no way shows the extent of my gratitude for this.*

• *You held me all evening after I had some major oral surgery done and the dentist didn't give me any pain medicine.*

• *You let me know that it was OK to stand up for what I believe in. I had signed a petition in school saying the Pledge of Allegiance should not be compulsory in class each morning. Tim and Mom had me in tears that evening as they chastised me for signing and for not being patriotic enough. You have no idea how relieved I was when you got home that night and told me that I had every right to sign that petition.*

• *You chose Marguerite Pappert for your wife. In retrospect, this has proven to be an excellent decision.*

All of my love,

Jill

Conclusion

Over the last few years, I have been one of the many Americans captivated by the resurging interest in angels. I was one of those thousands in stores browsing through angels books.

I believe angels exist - everywhere. They inspire others to carry on when times are tough; they encourage others to do their best; give their time and love to help their families, friends and communities; or are people who dare to step in and help a stranger in crisis.

Daniel, my given name, was the first prophet in the Bible to call any of the angels by name. It is in the book of Daniel that Michael and Gabriel meet by name and that we hear of the guardian angels of nations for the first time.

Gabriel came to Daniel to help him interpret dreams; when the king threw Daniel into the lion's den, an angel shut the lions' mouths. In the morning, when the den was opened, Daniel emerged unharmed.

Angels bring hope in times of despair. As I said earlier, I believe my own life has been spared nearly a half-dozen times by a higher power. Without divine intervention, there is no way I would be alive today.

I had excellent parents and much family support all through my life. Without their help, I would have never gotten through the last few years, not to mention graduating from college or anything else.

In June 1995, I met Victoria, the beautiful woman who is now my wife. It was a chance meeting at a concert that night. Angels must have guided Victoria and me.

Victoria needed a chair, so she asked to borrow the one next to me. I believe it was love at first sight for both of us. From the moment we introduced ourselves and touched, we have yet to let go of one another.

And to think I almost didn't go out on that early June South Carolina evening.

Victoria saved my life once with her quick thinking. We had been jogging one morning and were almost a mile away from my house when I suddenly fell incoherently to my knees because of low blood sugar. She could have panicked, but instead, she flagged down roadside assistance and got orange juice in my system to raise my blood sugar level. Thanks to her, in minutes, I was OK.

Victoria has always believed in me, even in times when I could not understand why. She loaned me the money for the publishing of my first book, *Life To The Fullest.* Times had been tough for me financially after relinquishing my publishing business in the late fall of 1994. I had a bag of bills to take care after the business closed and remained broke through 1995.

I remember coming back to my apartment one day in tears after discussions with a Raleigh, N.C., publisher. I told Victoria, "I don't know how I'll ever be published as an author. I know I won't be able to attract a national publisher because I haven't written any other books. I don't believe any of my books will go out to the American public because I cannot finance them. I know if I could get this first book out, I could help so many people with diabetes."

The next day, Victoria had a solution for me - she would loan me the money I needed to get started. I refused for a few weeks, but after her persistence, I took her up on the loan idea.

In my heart, I believed people would purchase the book and I could quickly return the money to her. My intuition was right; today, the diabetes book is being distributed through the United States and has been reviewed and approved by the national American Diabetes Association.

Another time, when South Carolina Press Association contest rolled around last fall, I was desperate. I had not allowed enough time to do the newspaper entries. Victoria stayed up nearly all night with me on consecutive nights, ensuring that I completed our entries. Then, we won the General Excellence Award for the state's best newspaper, along with awards for community service, best special section and best business reporting.

On June 8, 1996, Victoria, my best friend, love and personal angel, became my wife.

Throughout the last few years, I have met a succession of people who have changed my life for the better. I cannot even explain how I met this wonderful group of individuals, but I feel I had to have been led by a higher power. Without them, I would not have fulfilled my lifelong dream to become a published author, would not be healthy and likely would not even be alive.

Yes, I believe in everyday angels.

I am glad I have been able to tell these stories about the people in this book and how they impacted the lives of those around them. Most of us never do anything ultra-dramatic, but each of us has the opportunity to act as an angel - a true inspiration - in the lives of the people with whom we live, work and interact every day.

Do you believe?

If you do, you have the *chance* to be that everyday angel.

You have read about the
Collins Children's Home and its planned expansion
project in the pages of this book.
Approximately 150 child-care requests were submitted to
the home in 1995 alone. Those requests could not be granted
due to space limitations.

If you would like to help in the home's expansion, in
addition to the proceeds already allotted from this book,
please send a check or money order to:

Collins Children's Home
P.O. Box 745
Seneca, SC   29679-0745

For more information,
you can call Executive Director
Anne Rackley at
(864) 882-0893

Do You Know Other Angels?

━━━━━━━━━━

Many of the stories you have read here came from my experiences covering community news in four states. But I am willing to bet that you may know of an everyday angel. He or she may be the sort of person who gives back to his or her community, may have touched you in a personal way or even saved your life.

I am planning on doing a sequel to this book in the future. I would like to have your input. If you know of an everyday angel, drop me a line at the following address:

Dan Brannan
Dan Brannan Publications
P.O. Box 1708
Seneca, SC   29679
Phone: (864) 985-1300
Fax: (864) 271-1399

We will be sure to give you credit for your submissions and ideas - and thanks for your input and contributions. Please be sure to include the names, full addresses and phone numbers of the angel submissions. If you can, enclose a clear photograph, either black and white or color, of your everyday angel.

Want to order some more copies?

To order additional copies of
***Everyday Angels*,**
just send a check or money order to:

Dan Brannan Publications
P.O. Box 1708
Seneca, SC 29679

Name:_____

Address:_____

City, State, ZIP Code:_____

The book is $10.95 per copy, plus $3 postage and
handling for the first copy
Please enclose 50 cents per
additional copy of the book requested.
S.C. residents add 5 percent sales tax

FOR QUANTITY DISCOUNTS, WRITE:

Marketing Director
Dan Brannan Publications
P.O. Box 1708
Seneca, SC 29679

Tear here

Want to order some more copies?

To order additional cop: s of
Everyday Angels,
just send a check or money order to:

**Dan Brannan Publications
P.O. Box 1708
Seneca, SC   29679**

Name:_____

Address:_____

City, State, ZIP Code:_____

**The book is $10.95 per copy, plus $3 postage and
handling for the first copy
Please enclose 50 cents per
additional copy of the book requested.
S.C. residents add 5 percent sales tax**

FOR QUANTITY DISCOUNTS, WRITE:

**Marketing Director
Dan Brannan Publications
P.O. Box 1708
Seneca, SC   29679**

Tear here

Want to order some more copies?

To order additional copies of
Everyday Angels,
just send a check or money order to:

Dan Brannan Publications
P.O. Box 1708
Seneca, SC   29679

Name:_____

Address:_____

City, State, ZIP Code:_____

The book is $10.95 per copy, plus $3 postage and
handling for the first copy
Please enclose 50 cents per
additional copy of the book requested.
S.C. residents add 5 percent sales tax

FOR QUANTITY DISCOUNTS, WRITE:

Marketing Director
Dan Brannan Publications
P.O. Box 1708
Seneca, SC   29679

Tear here